OCTOBER 1977   Volume 28/Number 6

AMERICAN HERITAGE

Editor, Alvin M. Josephy, Jr.

Managing Editor, Geoffrey C. Ward

Art Director, Emma Landau

Board of Editors, E. M. Halliday, *Chairman;*
Nat Brandt, Bruce Catton, Barbara Klaw,
Elizabeth Oettinger, T. H. Watkins

Picture Editors, Devorah K. Cohen,
Carla Davidson, Mary Dawn Earley

Copy Editor, Brenda Savard

Editorial Assistant, Mary Elizabeth Wise

Contributing Editors, Allan L. Damon,
Oliver Jensen, Joan Paterson Kerr,
Richard F. Snow, Bernard A. Weisberger

Advisory Board, Henry Steele Commager,
Marshall B. Davidson, John A. Garraty,
Eugene D. Genovese, William H.
Goetzmann, Archibald Hanna, Howard H.
Peckham, Arthur M. Schlesinger, Jr.

London Office, Rosemary L. Klein

Design Consultant, Massimo Vignelli

AMERICAN HERITAGE
PUBLISHING COMPANY

Chairman of the Board, Samuel P. Reed
President and Publisher, Rhett Austell
Editor in Chief—Magazines, Alvin M.
Josephy, Jr.
Executive Editor—Magazines, Nat Brandt
Consulting Editor, J. H. Plumb
Editorial Art Director, Murray Belsky
Treasurer, Anthony J. Sansiveri
Promotion Director, Ernest S. Quick
Promotion Art Director, David A. Van Inwegen
Circulation and Sales Director, Donald B.
Barrows, Jr.
Production Director, Elbert Burr

Sponsored by American Association
for State and Local History · Society
of American Historians

AMERICAN HERITAGE, The Magazine of History,
is published every two months by American Heritage
Publishing Co., Inc.; editorial and executive offices,
10 Rockefeller Plaza, N.Y., N.Y. 10020. Secretary,
Anthony J. Sansiveri. Correspondence about
subscriptions should go to American Heritage
Subscription Office, 383 West Center St., Marion,
Ohio 43302. Single copies: $6. Annual subscriptions:
$21 in U.S.; $23 in Canada; $26 elsewhere. A 10-year
Index of Vols. VI-XV is available at $7.50; 5-year
Index of Vols. XVI-XX at $7.50; 5-year Index of Vols.
XXI-XXV at $7.50.

AMERICAN HERITAGE considers but assumes no
responsibility for unsolicited materials; these require
return postage. Title registered U.S. Patent Office.
Second-class postage paid at New York, N.Y., and at
additional mailing offices.

Postmaster: Please send Form 3579 to AMERICAN
HERITAGE, 381 West Center Street, Marion, Ohio
43302.

AMERICAN HERITAGE has been selected by the
Library of Congress for reproduction on recordings
called Talking Books, distributed free by regional
libraries in the U.S. to those unable to use
conventional print because of a visual or physical
handicap. For information write the Library of
Congress, Division for the Blind and Physically
Handicapped, 1291 Taylor St., N.W., Washington,
D.C. 20542.

THE
SWEDISH NIGHTINGALE
WALTZ.

CONTENTS

COVERS

Ever since Lewis and Clark, the grizzly bear has suffered a
terrible press. The slavering monster on our front cover
(a detail of the painting by William Leigh on pages 22-23) is
typical. The bear himself was both more and less than
his reputation, a fact made clear in the article beginning on
page 16—and by the real-life beast on our back cover.
FRONT COVER: THE THOMAS GILCREASE INSTITUTE OF AMERICAN HISTORY AND ART, TULSA,
OKLA. BACK COVER: PERRY SHANKLE, JR.

FRONTISPIECE

When the Swedish singer Jenny Lind came to America in
1850 under the auspices of P. T. Barnum, she enjoyed a
success unprecedented in the history of American
performing arts. For details of her conquest of America
and of her curious partnership with Barnum, see page 98.
HARVARD THEATRE COLLECTION

THE TIME OF THE ANGEL

The U-2, Cuba, and the CIA

by Don Moser

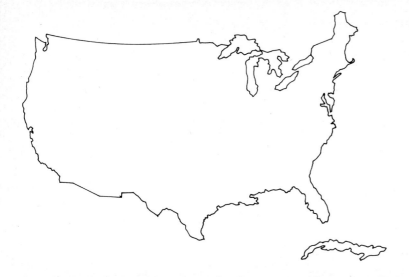

In the still of the October night, the slender, birdlike plane lifted into the sky from its base in California, climbed sharply on a column of flame, and headed east through the darkness. Pilot Richard Heyser, in the cramped, tiny cockpit, had good reason to be apprehensive, but he had little time to worry. He was totally occupied with the intricacies of navigation and with the exacting task of keeping his sleek aircraft aloft; for this plane was so specialized, so refined, that in the rarefied atmosphere that was its element it hung in the sky only tentatively, as if suspended from a wisp of spider's silk. As the plane climbed above fifty thousand feet it entered a critical altitude level called the "chimney." Once in the chimney, if the pilot flew a shade too slow, the plane would go into a stall and a spin from which it would never recover. If he flew a shade too fast, the fragile craft would come apart in mid-air.

For several hours the aircraft arrowed across the continent, gradually climbing higher and higher into the chimney. Periodically the pilot adjusted his airspeed, for as the plane climbed, the razor's edge between stall and disintegration grew ever finer, sharper. Dawn came, then sunrise. Now the Gulf of Mexico shimmered below.

The island came into view, tropical green rimmed by bright sand beaches. The pilot flew south of the island to a predetermined point in space, then turned back north. Pursuit might come at any time now, quick death slanting upward like an arrow.

There was a switch on a panel at his right hand. He had already thrown it from "off" to "stand by." Now as the plane passed high over the island's shore the pilot looked into his drift sight, a periscopelike device that peered through the belly of the plane. Then his hand moved once again to the switch on the panel. . .

During a period of thirteen days in October, 1962, the United States and the Soviet Union stood at the brink of war. In a confrontation over Russia's placing nuclear-tipped strategic missiles in Cuba, American aircraft, naval vessels, and assault troops went on alert and prepared for battle, while in Cuba Soviet technicians rushed to complete the installation of missiles that could reach almost any point in the United States. During the two-week crisis, President Kennedy estimated that the chance of armed conflict was "between one in three and even." Of course that potentially catastrophic war did not occur. Kennedy took a threatening stance and imposed a naval blockade; Soviet premier Khrushchev ultimately backed down, and the missiles were dismantled and returned to Russia.

As the missile crisis unfolded, a critical factor was Kennedy's certainty, beyond any shadow of doubt, that nuclear missiles were indeed being installed just a hundred miles from American shores. Kennedy was certain enough to take the grave risk of imposing a blockade—in itself an act of war—certain enough to contemplate the even graver risk of launching an air strike against Cuba, an act that might well have brought Soviet retaliation. How could Kennedy have been so *sure?*

The answer lies in a secret airplane flight and in the technology that made it possible—a technology of spying developed under the aegis of the Central Intelligence Agency. This technology wrapped American spies in a new cloak, ending the Mata Hari era and ushering in an age of optics and electronics. The technology also gave the U.S. an enormous intelligence-gathering advantage over the Soviet Union at the height of the Cold War. At times, as in the missile crisis, this intelligence allowed the U.S. to anticipate threatening moves by Russia. Equally important, the intelligence also dispelled groundless fears about Russian military superiority. Given the touchy temperament of the times, had the U.S. not possessed such intelligence, events might have taken an even more frightening turn.

The development of sophisticated intelligence-gathering tools began in the early 1950's, a time when the climate for such development was very favorable. For one thing, the President of the United States was a former general of the Army who had a professional soldier's familiarity with photographic intelligence. During World War II, aerial reconnaissance had been carried out by ordinary bombers and fighters stripped down and equipped with cameras instead of guns. These unarmed planes were highly vulnerable and extremely unpopular with their pilots, whose motto could be paraphrased as: "Get your pictures and get your tail out of there." The recon planes had to fly at low altitudes in turbulent air; since the cameras had no gyrostabilizing mechanisms to cushion them against shock, the quality of the photographs was generally poor, and even the quantity of information was limited by the film, which had a thick, space-consuming backing. In spite of these shortcomings, postwar analysis revealed that some 80 per cent of all useful military intelligence

Kennedy explains his stand . . .
U.P.I.

. . . and Castro explains his.
WIDE WORLD

came from aerial reconnaissance photographs.

Dwight Eisenhower entered the Presidency with a strong bias toward photographic reconnaissance. He felt that the intelligence-gathering services of the U.S. placed far too much reliance on "humint" (the spy trade's term for intelligence gathered from human sources) and "sigint" (the interception of radio and other electronic signals). Humint was prone to errors of judgment, bias, and exaggeration. As for sigint, most sensitive radio traffic was encrypted, and thus had to be decoded. Photographs neither lied nor required code-breaking.

Another factor made the time ripe for a breakthrough in the techniques of spying. In recruiting agents during the war, the Office of Strategic Services—the CIA's predecessor—had turned to the academic community, particularly to Ivy League and other prestigious universities. The reason was simple enough: the OSS needed people who had traveled abroad and who had proficiency in foreign languages; with the U.S. just emerging from the Depression, only the highly educated were apt to have such experience. This alliance of spies and scholars remained intact during the Eisenhower and Kennedy years, indeed remained intact until the academic community grew disillusioned over the war in Vietnam and over revelations of assassination plots and other dirty tricks carried out by the CIA.

Then of course there was the Cold War itself. During the early 1950's there was widespread concern about Russian nuclear superiority. In 1953 the Soviet Union exploded a hydrogen bomb. Shortly afterward it became clear that the Russians were working on the production of long-range aircraft, and in 1955 they unveiled an intercontinental bomber, the Bison, which was capable of striking the U.S. The Russians took pains to suggest that they were far along in their bomber program by skipping numbers in the serial designations on the planes they publicly displayed. When Western observers saw planes numbered, say, 19 and 21, they assumed that there was a bomber number 20, which did not in fact exist.

At the time, the U.S. had no reliable way of determining whether or not the Soviet Union had achieved superiority in nuclear weapons and delivery vehicles. Grasping at straws, American spies launched camera-carrying balloons that soared across Russia at sixty thousand feet or more, and then, over western Europe, dropped their camera mechanisms by para-chute—with luck into the hands of waiting intelligence agents. But some of the spy balloons went astray, and others drifted down inside Russia where they provided grist for Soviet propaganda. In any case, the balloon cameras produced pictures that, while adequate for making maps, did not provide enough detail to enlighten the U.S. about Russian weapons development.

Eisenhower was appalled at the lack of sound information about Russian capabilities. Thus in 1954 he created a special presidential committee to study the subject of surprise attack. Chaired by James Killian, the president of MIT, the committee was charged with determining whether or not the U.S. might be facing another Pearl Harbor. At a meeting in the fall, the committee decided that the U.S. should begin reconnaissance overflights of Russia and the Soviet-bloc countries.

The only problem was that no aircraft existed that could carry out such a mission. But in the course of its investigations the committee learned that a conceptual design for a high-altitude reconnaissance plane had recently been submitted to the Air Force by Clarence "Kelly" Johnson, the chief aircraft designer for Lockheed. Johnson's proposed design was so extraordinary that the Air Force turned it down on the grounds that such a plane simply could not be built. But the President's committee was more sanguine, and they passed on their views to Eisenhower, who immediately told Allen Dulles, then head of the CIA, to get that airplane built—urgently and secretly.

Dulles appointed one of his top deputies, Richard Bissell, to ramrod the project. A recent CIA recruit, Bissell was an economist who had taught on the faculty of Yale and MIT, and who had served as an administrator in the Marshall Plan. Bissell started things moving that very day. With an opposite number from the Air Force, he hatched a scheme to finance the project secretly. The CIA had a special reserve fund for which it had to make no specific accounting. From this fund the agency would pay for the air-frame development. The Air Force already had on order a large number of Pratt and Whitney engines that could power the Lockheed design. The Air Force would buy a few more engines and bury the extras in their larger order. Financing settled, Bissell phoned Kelly Johnson at Lockheed and told him to get to work.

Kelly Johnson was a shy, chubby genius who looked rather like W. C. Fields, and whose idea of recreation was working calculus

*Above: Clarence "Kelly" Johnson,
brilliant designer of the U-2, at the
wingtip of one model, ca. 1962. Right:
Tony Levier, Lockheed test pilot, who was
the first man to fly the extraordinary
new airplane when it was built in 1954.*
ABOVE: LOCKHEED. RIGHT: LOS ANGELES *Times*

problems. He was probably the most brilliant aircraft designer alive. During his long career he created the famous P-38 of World War II, the F-80, which was America's first jet fighter; the C-130 Hercules, which is still an Air Force cargo workhorse; the F-104 Starfighter; and the high-altitude SR-71. A man who liked to work with a compact staff and a minimum of fuss and red tape, his stature with Lockheed was such that he had almost total autonomy. Now he hand-picked a small team of twenty-three engineers and technicians and moved them into a Lockheed hangar in Burbank, California—a secret workshop that Johnson named "the Skunk Works," after the spot in Dogpatch where Hairless Joe brewed up his famous Kickapoo Joy Juice.

It was no wonder the Air Force had considered the plane impossible to build. To be safe from interception it had to fly at an altitude of seventy thousand feet—some twenty-five thousand feet above the operating ceilings of contemporary aircraft. In the thin air at that altitude, a jet engine would barely run at all, and it would produce only 6 per cent of its sea-level thrust. The plane had to stay in the air for over ten hours and cruise as far as a B-52, and its fuel capacity was so limited that it had to get an incredibly efficient five miles per gallon of fuel while flying at five hundred miles per hour. And since the crash landing of a spy plane on foreign soil would have serious diplomatic repercussions, the new aircraft had to be highly reliable.

Under tight security, Johnson's team went to work on the project, which was code-named "Aquatone." The plane that soon took shape in the Skunk Works was a marvel of elegant simplicity, a sleek machine with an eighty-foot span of slender, tapering wings. It looked more like a glider than a conventional airplane, and indeed from seventy thousand feet it would glide for three hundred miles before touching the earth. Johnson's engineers struggled to pare away every ounce of excess weight. They designed a wing that weighed only three pounds per square foot—a third that of a normal aircraft. They attached the tail assembly to the fuselage with just three bolts. They designed the canopy above the cockpit to be operated by hand. Instead of heavy conventional landing gear the plane had "pogos"—tiny wheels suspended from the wingtips by slender rods. On takeoff, the pogos dropped off as soon as the plane was airborne. On landing, the pilot coasted in on a belly wheel and lightweight skids on the wingtips. Disassembled, the entire plane could be stowed away in

a cargo aircraft or transported to a take-off point by truck.

The plane would ultimately become known as the U-2. But the men in the Skunk Works had a nickname of their own for the graceful machine they were creating. They called it "the Angel."

As the first Angels were built in the Skunk Works, Bissell, Kelly Johnson, and Lockheed test pilot Tony Levier armed themselves with topographical maps and made scouting flights over the western deserts, looking for a location so remote that the Angel could be test flown in total secrecy. Finally they found a dry lake bed that could serve as a landing strip. Now roads had to be built, a well dug, hangars and living quarters erected at the hidden site. The construction crews who did this job had no idea what they were working on, and indeed everything about the Angel was shrouded in secrecy. In discussions the plane was known as "the article," the pilot was called "the driver," and the secret desert base was called "home plate." In Burbank, disassembled Angels were loaded into covered trucks, which pulled out at dusk and traveled to "home plate" during the night.

On August 6, 1955, just under eight months from the day that Kelly Johnson got the go-ahead from Bissell, the Angel was ready to fly. On its first taxi test the plane popped thirty-six feet into the air—with its ultralight construction and enormous wingspan, the Angel simply wanted to fly. When Tony Levier took the plane up on its first flight, he had to try five times before he could force the eager Angel back to earth.

Until the pilots got accustomed to the plane, the Angel's determination to stay airborne caused them considerable difficulty. There were other snags too. Condensation formed on the faceplates of the pilots' pressure suits, blurring their vision, and the Pratt and Whitney engine that powered the plane proved subject to flameouts at high altitudes. Before all these problems were solved, one Angel crashed, a second disintegrated, and a third disappeared along with its pilot.

Eventually the difficulties were overcome. Angels started making long endurance flights to the Canadian border and back, to the Tennessee mountains and back. A training program was set up for pilots, both "blue suiters" (Air Force officers) and "the other guys" (men from the CIA). These pilots were an elite group. Candidates had to have a thousand hours of single-engine time even to be considered for the U-2 program. Of those accepted,

Above, left: the U-2 camera. Left: "Automat," the secret photo-interpretation center in Washington, D.C. Above: Art Lundahl, master photo-interpreter.
ALL: CIA

A Soviet freighter heads for Cuba carrying crated guided-missile patrol boats in August, 1962. Such pictures, although not taken by U-2s, convinced American intelligence experts that U-2 flights over Cuba must be made.
U.S. NAVY

many had problems with the special pressure suits they had to wear at high altitude. These garments were so precisely fitted that if a pilot gained or lost two pounds, his suit was useless. And the suit forced a pilot to breathe artificially; that is, he had to consciously suck in a breath—then the suit would force him to expel the air. Before they could fly the tricky U-2, the pilots spent hours in pressure chambers, learning to breath this way naturally and unconsciously. Some simply could not acquire the knack, and perhaps half the trainees washed out for this reason.

Even as the Angel was under construction and the pilots were being trained, other components necessary for a spy plane were being rushed to completion. Among the breakthroughs was a new Mylar-based film developed by Eastman Kodak. Hardly thicker than Saran Wrap, this film could be loaded into a compact aerial camera in enormous quantities. Another crucial component was a revolutionary new lens designed by Dr. James Baker, a Harvard astronomer. The resolving power, or sharpness, of a lens is measured by the number of lines it can distinguish per millimeter. World War II aerial lenses could resolve from twelve to fifteen lines. Baker's new lens could distinguish from fifty to sixty lines. When mounted in a telephoto camera in an airplane flying at an altitude of about eight miles, the Baker lens could read the headlines on a newspaper lying on the ground. At thirteen miles, it could see an object the size of a sport jacket. Not only was this lens superior to anything that had existed before, but it could now be produced in quantity, and quickly. Previously, lenses had to be ground by hand—a laborious, slow process. But now, in the new electronics age, computers could take over the task of lens making.

Something else was needed: a new camera. With Dr. Edwin Land, the innovative head of Polaroid, functioning as a general catalyst, a series of camera designs were created by the Hycon Corporation, a California optical company. Chief among these was the "B-camera." This rapid-fire machine swung its lens from side to side, producing strips of pictures that, when overlapped, formed a stereo image. Weighing 450 pounds, the camera was designed to fit snugly into the slender fuselage of the U-2.

There was still one more ingredient necessary for a completed spy system: someone had to make expert sense out of the enormous quantity of photographic intelligence that the U-2 would soon be bringing home. In 1953 the CIA had acquired just

such an expert in Art Lundahl, a teacher of photo-interpretation from the University of Chicago. A friendly, ebullient man with boundless enthusiasm for his arcane craft, Lundahl had worked on the Bikini atom bomb tests, determining from photos the damage done to ships that were still too radioactive for close-up inspection. He was a master both of photo-interpretation—the qualitative art of identifying photographed objects—and photogrammetry—the quantitative art of determining their dimensions.

In Washington, Lundahl set up a small photo-intelligence unit, and in December, 1954, he got a cryptic phone call from Allen Dulles' office, relieving him of all duties and telling him to report to the director immediately. He met with Dulles and Richard Bissell, who unveiled the plans for the U-2 and told Lundahl to establish a photo-interpretation shop capable of handling large quantities of film. He was to keep what he was doing an absolute secret—not even his immediate supervisor was to know what he was up to.

Lundahl set up his laboratory in the last place anyone would think to look—above an auto repair shop in a seedy section of Southeast Washington. He and his team kicked their way through garbage to get to work and risked muggings on their way home, but they had plenty of room and a high degree of inconspicuousness. Lundahl foresaw the day when his lab would be able to provide an unprecedented amount and variety of information to suit any intelligence appetite, and so he gave his operation an appropriate code name: Automat.

Plane, film, lens, camera, interpretation—the greatest intelligence-gathering tool in history was now complete. From a height of thirteen miles the U-2 could photograph a swath of country 750 miles wide, about 150 miles of that in high-resolution stereo. Carrying twelve thousand feet of film in its magazines, the plane could scan a path from Washington to Phoenix in a single flight. And in just twelve missions, the inquisitive Angel could gather all significant information on a land mass the size of the United States.

The first U-2 flight over Russia took place on July 4, 1956. By the second or third mission the Russians had picked up the plane on their radar, which was more sophisticated than U.S. analysts had thought, but the Soviets had no weapon capable of bringing down the high-flying intruder. For four years the Angels criss-

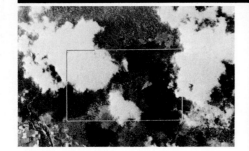

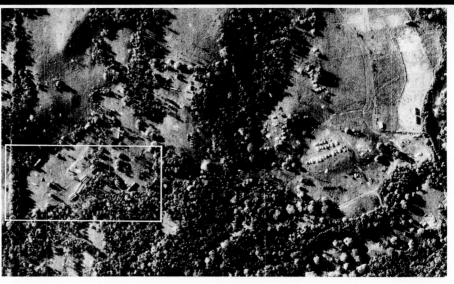

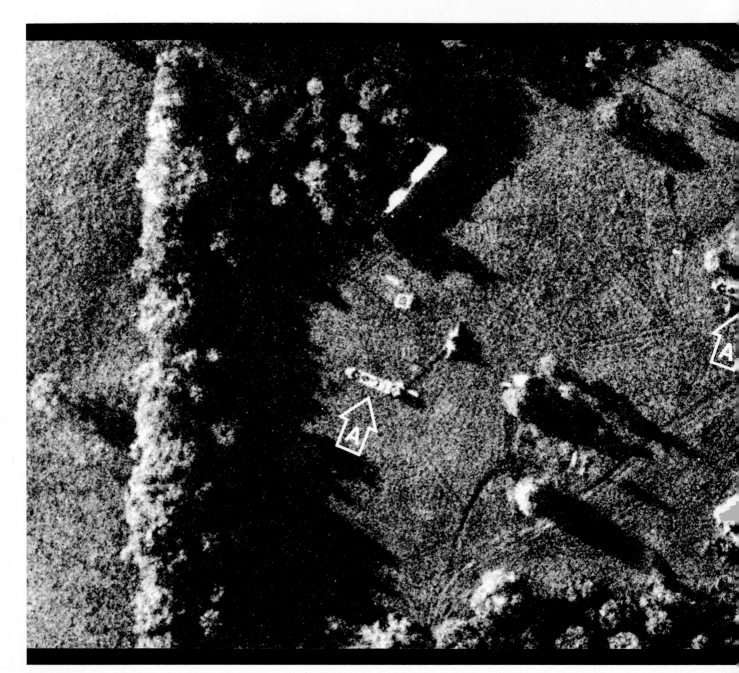

These photographs, taken by U-2s flying over Cuba, demonstrate the amazing perspicacity of the plane's camera, as well as the hard evidence on which President Kennedy made his decision to "quarantine" the island. The small prints, far left and immediate left, are shots taken in August, 1962; the first shows no military activity in the San Cristóbal area, but the other, of the La Coloma region, shows disturbing indications of SAM sites. On October 14, a flight directly over San Cristóbal produced the picture shown in the middle print at left; a detail of this (outlined area), enlarged below, clearly reveals erector-launcher equipment (A), missile trailers (B), and missile shelter tents (C).

LEFT TO RIGHT: U.P.I., U.S. AIR FORCE, CIA. BELOW: CIA

With the announcement of the quarantine, President Kennedy put Air Force, Navy, and Marine Corps units on stand-by alert pending the reaction of the Soviet Union. Left: jet fighters at Patrick Air Force Base in Florida, ready for action.
U.P.I.

crossed the Russian skies, until May 1, 1960, when a U-2 piloted by Francis Gary Powers was shot down over Russia by a SAM—a surface-to-air missile. The Powers incident brought a storm of protest from Russia, and resulted in a cessation of overflights. But in those four years the spy planes had gathered an enormous amount of information. First they had proved that a "bomber gap" did not exist; the Russians were not ahead of the U.S. in long-range bomber capacity. Later, they proved that the much-feared "missile gap" did not exist either.

But the ultimate employment of the U-2 was not to occur for two more years, during the administration of John Kennedy. In the summer of 1962 it became evident that Russia was sending massive arms shipments to Cuba. The U.S. intelligence community had a worldwide ship-watching network, and as Russian vessels passed through choke points like the Bosporus, U.S. military attachés in Istanbul simply stood on the shore, observed the ships, and photographed them. Many of the ships had large crates on their decks, and these were a dead giveaway, for back at Automat Lundahl's interpreters had developed a new skill they called "cratology"—which was the science of deducing the identity of objects concealed inside crates. For years CIA agents had been observing the kinds of packages the Russians used to wrap their military equipment. During May Day festivals in Moscow, when the Soviets traditionally paraded their new weapons, agents observed and photographed missiles, tanks, planes, and other hardware. Now when photographs of the Russian deck cargo arrived in Washington, Lundahl's photo-grammetry experts needed only a single known dimension—such as, say, the height of a deckhand—to measure accurately every-thing else in view. By August some seventy-five Soviet or Soviet-chartered ships had reached Cuba or were en route, and the cratologists had determined that they were transporting missile-carrying PT boats, cruise missiles, MIG fighters, and other sophisticated weapons.

Along with this evidence, the CIA was also gathering a great deal of "humint" on the Cuba buildup—too much of it, in fact. At the time, refugees were pouring out of Cuba and into Miami. The new arrivals were taken to Task Force W, a CIA debriefing station established at Opa-Locka, Florida. There they were interrogated by Spanish-speaking analysts; those who seemed to have useful information were held for further questioning. The

refugees were full of gossip, rumors, hysteria, and a generalized hatred of the Castro regime that caused them to see apocalypse around every corner. They flooded the system with reports of SAMs and nuclear missiles. Again and again these reports proved false. (Indeed, by January of 1962, months before the arms shipments began, the CIA had received 211 refugee reports of missiles in Cuba.) Confronted with so much bad information, so much "background noise," the CIA's intelligence analysts became skeptical about all refugee reports.

Intelligence from agents in Cuba would have been more reliable, but such intelligence was in short supply in 1962. Following the Bay of Pigs, Castro had declared a "war on traitors," rounding up thousands of Cubans with doubtful loyal-ties; among them were most of the CIA's Cuban spies. With those informants lost, analysts had no way of corroborating the refugee reports.

Harder information was needed—the kind that could be provided only by the U-2. A mission was flown, and when the film was inspected on August 29, Lundahl's interpreters saw some-thing new, and sinister—the familiar Star of David pattern of a Russian SAM site. Indeed, in ensuing days they found eight such sites under construction. The key question was: were the SAMs simply part of an antiaircraft defense system, or did their presence have more menacing implications? Could they be there to protect other missiles—nuclear missiles?

The discovery of the SAMs caused consternation in the White House, but on September 4 Khrushchev sent a message via Russian ambassador Dobrynin to Robert Kennedy, for relay to the President. The message said, in effect, that Khrushchev had no intention of creating any problems for Kennedy during 1962, an election year. In response, Kennedy issued a public warning that if offensive missiles were introduced into Cuba, "the gravest issues would arise." A few days later, the Kremlin made another mollifying statement indicating that there was no plan for installing missiles in Cuba.

Most members of the American intelligence community accepted the Russian denials—not because of faith in the Krem-lin's honesty, but because it simply did not seem rational for the Russians to place offensive nuclear missiles in Cuba. They had never placed such missiles in Soviet-bloc countries in Europe, although they could have done so with impunity. Why would they

At Guantánamo, the big American naval base at Cuba's eastern end, ships and planes performed "exercises" during the crisis, while Marines in fighting gear awaited orders to move.
BOTH: ROBERT W. KELLEY. *Life* MAGAZINE © TIME, INC.

now place them in the Caribbean, where the U.S. was sure to regard their presence as extremely provocative, and where the U.S. had total military superiority? Cuba was important to Russia; the United States had already backed one botched invasion of the country. Why provide the Americans with an excuse to launch an all-out attack?

Certainly it was plausible that the Kremlin believed it necessary to beef up Cuba's antiaircraft defenses. The U.S. had supported the Bay of Pigs attack the previous year, and the CIA had been busily hatching bizarre schemes for doing away with Castro. The U.S. also had allowed some publicity about a forthcoming military exercise planned for the Caribbean in the fall of 1962. This operation, code-named "Philbriglex-62," was to involve an assault by seventy-five hundred Marines, heavily supported by aircraft carriers and other vessels, on an island off the coast of Puerto Rico. According to the scenario, the Marines were to "liberate" a small country called Vieques from a dictator named Ortsac—which, of course, is Castro spelled backward. Russia was aware of this operation, and might reasonably have suspected it was a practice run for the real thing.

There were some dissenters from the generally sanguine outlook shared by most U.S. intelligence experts. Chief among these was John McCone, who had taken over from Allen Dulles as head of the CIA in the aftermath of the Bay of Pigs fiasco. McCone, who always took the dimmest possible view of Russian intent, felt that the Kremlin might indeed install offensive missiles as bargaining chips for future negotiations. McCone accounted for the fact that Russia had not given such missiles to its eastern European allies on the ground that Russia did not trust its satellites, and feared the missiles might be turned back on Moscow. Placed in Cuba, medium-range ballistic missiles could not reach back to Russia. But they could reach the United States.

The truth could best be learned through the hard data produced by more overhead reconnaissance. But now there was an obstacle to sending the Angels winging over Cuba. With SAMs now in place in Cuba, there was a strong possibility of losing a plane, and the resulting international uproar could severely limit the future use of America's most effective spying tool. The Committee on Overhead Reconnaissance, made up of representatives from the CIA and various military intelligence branches, finally decided on a compromise course. They would send the U-2s on "sheep-dipping" missions—that is, the planes would fly off the island's shore, briefly dipping inland to take quick photographic peeks, then hightailing it away. None would fly directly over the western end of Cuba, where the SAMs were being installed.

The sheep-dipping flights failed to turn up any new evidence, and on September 19 the U.S. Intelligence Board met in Washington to try to draw some conclusions. The board, made up of members from the CIA, the National Security Council, and the State and Defense Departments, weighed all available evidence and advised the President that it was extremely unlikely that the Russians were installing strategic nuclear missiles. Pessimistic as always, John McCone, who was honeymooning on the Riviera, cabled his dissent.

But no sooner had the board reported to the President than new information surfaced—information with disturbing overtones. For one thing, large-hatched ships were seen arriving in Cuba. Ordinarily these ships were used for transporting such bulk cargo as lumber, but the vessels approaching Cuba were riding high in the water, as if carrying light but bulky loads. Then intelligence analysts received a report that Fidel Castro's personal pilot had drunkenly boasted that "We will fight to the death and perhaps we can win because we have everything, including atomic weapons." On September 21, two days after the Intelligence Board meeting, a crucial report finally reached Washington: nine days earlier, a CIA agent in Havana had spotted a truck carrying what appeared to be a shrouded long-range missile. The agent managed to get onto a refugee flight to Florida, where he met with intelligence analysts. His sketches of the truck's rear profile and other information he gave suggested that the truck was indeed carrying a large strategic missile. Corroboration for his story followed quickly, with another report that similarly laden vehicles had been seen in the area of San Cristóbal, about fifty miles southwest of Havana.

There was yet another worrisome bit of intelligence: Colonel John Wright, an analyst with the Defense Intelligence Agency, had carefully studied the earlier U-2 photos of the SAM installations. There was something peculiar about the SAM sites in the San Cristóbal area: the missiles were laid out in a pattern similar to that the Russians had used when setting up defenses for strategic missile sites in the U.S.S.R.

By October 4, the accumulated evidence was so suggestive that

At an emergency session of the United Nations Security Council on October 25, the U.S.A. shows convincing U-2 evidence; Ambassador Zorin of the U.S.S.R. (behind "President" sign) ignores it.
NEAL BOENZI. THE *New York Times*

the Committee on Overhead Reconnaissance decided to authorize a U-2 flight over the San Cristóbal area, in spite of the considerable risks involved. But instead of launching a spy plane immediately, the intelligence community now got involved in a time-consuming bureaucratic squabble over which agency should run the operation, the CIA or the Air Force. In case the plane was shot down—and that was a strong possibility—the difference would be by no means academic. If the pilot was a CIA man he could be treated as a spy, even shot. But under what is known in the spy trade as the "theory of plausible denial," the U.S. could disavow any connection with the mission. While such a disavowal would be a transparent fiction, it would have a certain diplomatic utility. On the other hand, if the pilot was an Air Force officer the overflight could be construed as an act of war.

For these reasons, sensitive missions such as the one now planned were customarily flown by CIA pilots. In this case, however, with actual armed conflict now a clear possibility, the Air Force lobbied for the right to fly the mission, and eventually won out. The pilot would, however, fly a CIA plane, for the agency's U-2s were souped-up models carrying electronic countermeasures against SAMs.

More time was lost because of cloud cover over Cuba, but finally, on October 14, Mission G3101 Victor was launched. Major Richard Heyser, the pilot, was a 35-year-old Floridian. An experienced flier, he was an old friend of Francis Gary Powers, and he was skilled in a variety of maneuvers designed for evading SAMs. Just in case he was shot down he carried plenty of Air Force identification to ensure that he was not treated as a spy. He did not carry cyanide pills or other suicide devices. If captured and interrogated, he would divulge no more information than necessary, but he was not expected to remain silent in the face of torture.

About 8 A.M. on the fourteenth, Heyser approached Cuba from the south across the Isle of Pines. He passed over Cuba in six minutes, while the camera behind him in the fuselage, its lens rotating from position to position, took 928 photographs. No SAMs were fired at him. His work done, Heyser flew back to the U.S. and landed in Florida.

The film was rushed to Lundahl's Automat operation in the Washington slums, and the next morning, in a high-ceilinged room painted battleship gray, a team of photo-interpreters went

to work. Late that afternoon Lundahl got a call from one of his men. "We want you to come and look at something."

When Lundahl reached the room, the interpreters said nothing about what they had found, for it was customary in this business to let each man draw his own conclusions. Lundahl went to the light table, where he adjusted the twin stereoscopic eyepieces to suit his vision. There on the film he saw an area of palm trees and jungle vegetation slashed by the track marks of heavy equipment. In a clearing he saw empty missile transporters, blast deflectors, cherry-picker cranes, wires and cables strung along the ground. Most significantly, he saw rectangular tents designed to cover something very long and narrow, and some special vans like those the Russians used to transport nuclear warheads.

After examining the film carefully for five minutes, Lundahl turned to the interpreters and said, "OK, I know what you guys are thinking, and you're right. These are medium-range ballistic missiles. I don't want anyone to leave this room. Call your wives, break up your car pools. Do it casually. But stay in this room."

It was 5:30 P.M. Lundahl picked up a secure "gray phone" and called the CIA headquarters in Langley, Virginia. McCone was out of town attending a funeral, and Lundahl got Ray Cline, the agency's deputy director for intelligence. "Ray," he said, "sorry to break up your day, but we're looking at MRBMs going into Cuba, and even out here in the boondocks we know what that means."

Cline was dumbfounded. "Are you sure? You aren't imagining it?"

"I'm sure."

"I hope you're holding the ceiling on."

"I've got everybody buttoned up in the room."

"Don't go off half-cocked." Cline said. "Go back and do your homework again." After telling Lundahl to recheck the film, Cline faced an awkward couple of hours. The CIA was hosting its counterparts from England, Canada, and Australia at a Commonwealth intelligence conference in Washington, and Cline was expected to appear at a cocktail party that evening. He bluffed his way through the party, got home by eight, and talked once more to Lundahl, who confirmed the existence of the MRBMs. Lundahl had found two sites containing SS-4 missiles. Known to U.S. analysts as "Sandals," they had a range of 1,020

*As things calmed down, Soviet freighters
left Cuba carrying crated bombers (above,
left) and missile launchers (above); J.F.K.
gave Art Lundahl and others silver
souvenir calendars (left).*
CLOCKWISE FROM TOP LEFT: U.P.I., WIDE WORLD, ART LUNDAHL

nautical miles—which put them within striking distance of Washington, D.C.

Cline's first action was to call presidential assistant McGeorge Bundy at his home. Since he had no scrambler phone, Cline felt it necessary to be circumspect. "You know that island we were talking about a few days ago?" he said. "Well, they've got some big ones."

Bundy caught on immediately. He was staggered by the news. "Are they ready to shoot now?" he asked.

"No, but they are rapidly approaching it."

Next, Cline tried to alert the State Department. He reached Roger Hilsman, the department's chief of intelligence, at a cocktail party. Once again Cline described the missiles circumspectly, but this time his cryptic references were less effective. Hilsman thought he was talking about bombers, not missiles, and it took some time for Cline, using circumlocutions, to make himself understood. As soon as he hung up, Cline found out he wasn't so clever as he thought. His fourteen-year-old daughter, who had happened to be in the next room, came in and said, "Where are the missiles—in Cuba or China?"

Through the rest of Monday evening, other top-level officials of the government were tracked down at home or at social functions and were told the news. Meanwhile, all through the night, Lundahl's team kept checking the film over and over again. Everything they saw strengthened their convictions.

Early the next morning, McGeorge Bundy went to the White House and informed the President: "There is now hard photographic evidence that the Russians have offensive missiles in Cuba." Realizing that Khrushchev had lied to him, Kennedy reacted with surprise and anger. "He can't do that to *me*!"

Meanwhile, Lundahl and Cline were preparing their briefing for the President at the CIA's Langley headquarters. Just as they were walking out the door with a big black case full of photographs, a bus carrying the delegates to the Commonwealth intelligence conference pulled up. Cline, who was supposed to address the opening conference session that morning, was caught in an embarrassing spot—anyone could see that he was going off on some important errand. (Later, as the feverish comings and goings around Washington became increasingly obvious, Cline dropped hints that convinced the foreign intelligence officers that the crisis was over Berlin).

At the White House, Lundahl and Cline went to the Oval Office and spread the pictures out on the President's desk. Lundahl handed Kennedy a big Sherlock-Holmes-style magnifying glass and pointed out the incriminating evidence. Kennedy took a long time examining the pictures. Then he turned to Lundahl, fixed him with a hard stare, and said, "Are you sure?"

"It can be a papier-mâché world out there," Lundahl replied. "But I'm as sure of this as a photo-interpreter can be."

Over the following days there were more U-2 flights, and the photo-interpreters were able to pinpoint a total of six MRBM sites. They also found three sites for intermediate-range ballistic missiles, which could carry nuclear warheads for twenty-two hundred nautical miles to strike at any point in the United States except for a small section of the Pacific Northwest. At the United Nations when Adlai Stevenson accused the Russians of installing the missiles, Soviet Ambassador Zorin tried to deny their existence, but Lundahl's deputy was waiting in the wings with huge enlargements of the photographs. When he wheeled the pictures onto the floor of the Security Council, there was no contesting the evidence. Representatives of the CIA flew to the capitals of major Allied nations with copies of the pictures and convinced the foreign chiefs of state that the U.S. was acting on hard fact. Confronted by all this, Khrushchev ordered the missiles removed from Cuba. Later, when the Russians began to withdraw the missiles, U-2s confirmed that they were gone.

Today, of course, all this seems almost primitive, for things have changed a lot in the last fifteen years. The technology of spying is much advanced, with Russian and American satellites orbiting the earth and sending back intelligence from altitudes far beyond any achieved by the U-2.

John F. Kennedy and Nikita Khrushchev are gone—and most of the experts who played key roles in the development of the Angel and its associated technology are now fully or partly retired. But they must look back, from time to time, to a brief moment when it and they were in charge of history.

Don Moser, who was formerly an assistant managing editor of LIFE, is now a free-lance writer who lives in Washington, D.C. He is currently working on a book about the China-Burma-India theater in World War II.

URSUS HORRIBILIS IN EXTREMIS

The grizzly perceived: In 1911, William R. Leigh did these meticulous sketches of the bear from a model held captive in the Bronx Zoo. There is fierceness present here, and a raw power, but none of the imaginative distortion that transformed beast into monster in so many other paintings.

The Last Stand of King Grizzly

by John G. Mitchell

Bears and people have been at war for a long time—possibly longer than two predatory mammals should be, with any hope of mutual survival. In the beginning, the bears won almost every time, though not as often as the great cats did. Together with the great cats, bears provided spice to the human experience. People were obliged to defend themselves, were forced to *think*. Fires were lit at the mouth of the cave. Weapons were invented. Then the bears began to lose. People pictured them on the walls of caves. In some cultures, bears became as gods, and apologies were offered even as huntsmen plunged their lances through the bear's hide. Next, there were legends and tall tales at the campfires. Smokey put on his ranger hat. Gentle Ben smiled for the television camera. Soon, a few people began to root for the bear, or at least for a truce.

They offered renewed apologies even as they designated one kind of bear a threatened species throughout much of its historic range. This was *Ursus horribilis*, the great silvertip grizzly, the onetime scourge of mountain men and cowboys, the epicenter of the back-country camper's darkest dream, the largest, the deadliest, the most fearsome fang-and-claw critter on the North American continent.

It was a fine gesture, this effort to protect the bear, but late. Once, the grizzly ranged far and wide; east from the Pacific coast halfway to the Atlantic, and south to the Gulf of Mexico. But most are gone now. The grizzly was gone from California by 1922, from Utah by 1923, from Oregon and Arizona and New Mexico by 1935 or earlier; so long gone from the Dakotas that few citizens of those states are old enough to remember the last of the breed thereabouts. Though sizable and somewhat stable grizzly populations still prevail in Alberta, British Columbia, the Yukon, and Alaska, the bear's range in the coterminus United States is sharply pinched. It is about four hundred miles long and from one hundred to two hundred miles wide; it embraces Yellowstone and Glacier national parks, and spills somewhat questionably across the Idaho panhandle above Coeur d'Alene into the northeast corner of Washington State. Considering what used to be, that isn't much of a kingdom. Not for the grizzly, anyway.

In all likelihood, most of the 750 to one thousand grizzlies remaining in the Lower Forty-eight are confined to the near precincts of Glacier and Yellowstone parks, where, despite increasing human pressure on the back country, bears find fewer opportunities to test the marksmanship or trapping skills of people who still perceive predators darkly from the mouth of an ideological cave.

Rooting for bears, as I do, one has to believe that the grizzly deserves to find its own way to extinction, unhurried and unaided by humankind, like the brontosaur before it. But that kind of going is out of fashion these days; it is almost impossible when, on the one hand, you have a large animal capable of homicide, and on the other, ideological cavemen with high-powered rifles, builders of logging roads and condominium resorts, tenders of sheep and cows, miners of ores, and others who press their claims to some part of the bear's diminishing world. So the war goes on, protective rulings by the U.S. Fish and Wildlife Service notwithstanding.

To be sure, the nation will not perish should the grizzly disappear altogether. But something of importance will be missing nonetheless. I mean the cultural loss, the purging of risk and danger from a wilderness that is already safe enough for all but the errant fool. I believe that to qualify as wilderness a piece of country requires something special: a presence larger and stronger than a man, and wiser to the woods, and fully capable of killing. It is not essential that one encounter such a presence. It is enough to know that it is there.

The history of *Ursus horribilis* is a capsule history of the American West. No other single wild species—not even the wolf or the cougar—has figured quite so prominently in the literature of exploration and settlement beyond the hundredth meridian.

Paleontologists tell us that somewhere to the north and west is where it all began—likely in the early Pleistocene forests of Asia, in the form of a large brown bear since immortalized as *Ursus etruscus*. About thirty thousand years ago came great sheets of ice. The forest became sparse and coniferous. In some places taiga

18

and tundra took over. The bear adapted. *Ursus etruscus* became *Ursus arctos*. And one fine morning in Siberia, Arctos gazed out upon a shallow Bering Sea and saw a bridge of tundra reaching to America.

No doubt it took the bear many millennia to wander through what is now Alaska into the coastal ranges of the Northwest, to the Sierra Nevada, to the Rockies, to the parched hills of Mexico. With a preference for open country, the bear ranged eastward, moseying along the rich river bottoms of the Great Plains, growing fat on berries and ungulate prey. There is fossil evidence that some grizzlies crossed the Mississippi River and poked tentatively into the hardwood forests of Ohio. But mostly the species backed off and retreated with the sun, leaving the East to *Ursus americanus* (the black bear) and to the woodland Indians who would come later.

To what extent the early Indians of the West counted coup on Lord Grizzly—and vice versa—can only be conjectured. Bear hides and claw necklaces were worn or displayed by members of some tribes. The acquisition of such finery no doubt was costly. For the most part, the American Indian revered the great bear. Indeed, to some cultures it was a deity. Charles Fletcher Lummis, a newspaper correspondent who spent many years among the Indians of the Southwest in the late 1800's, reported that the Navajos were in mortal dread of the bear—not of its fangs and claws but of its imagined supernatural powers. There was only one excuse, wrote Lummis, for meddling with a grizzly. That was when a bear killed a Navajo. A large party of warriors and medicine men would proceed to the animal's lair. And then, as Lummis told it: "The praises of the bear, commander of beasts, are loudly sung, and his pardon is humbly invoked for the unpleasant deed to which they are now driven. Having duly apologized beforehand, they proceed as best they may to kill the bear, and then go home to fast and purify themselves."

Probably the first written account of the grizzly by a European was that of Father Antonio de la Ascensión, official scribe on the voyage of Sebastián Vizcaíno to Monterey Bay in 1602. The padre saw the bears feeding on a beached whale, and later, inspecting their tracks in the sand, noted that they measured "a good third of a yard long and a hand wide."

The first English observers were more observant. In 1691, the Hudson's Bay Company dispatched one Henry Kelsey on a thousand-mile journey from Fort York, at the mouth of the Nelson River, to the plains of western Saskatchewan. According to Kelsey's journal, he and his Assiniboin guide pitched their tent on August 20 and looked out upon a view affording "Nothing but short round sticky grass and buffalo and a great sort of a bear which is bigger than any white bear and is neither white nor black but silver hair'd like our English rabbit...." Later, the two men encountered a pair of grizzlies at close range and discovered that this great sort of a bear had something else in common with the English rabbit—a swiftness of foot. The grizzlies charged, chasing the Assiniboin up a tree and Kelsey into a thick clump of willows. From this implausible hiding place, Kelsey claimed he shot and killed both bears with his flintlock musket. The feat earned him the honorary title of "Little Giant" among the northern tribes, and possibly the dubious distinction of being the first white man ever to slay a grizzly.

A century after Kelsey's journey, Alexander Mackenzie set out from Montreal to complete the first overland crossing of America north of Mexico. In his journals, the Scot referred to "grisly and hideous bears," and recounted how "One of our men, being at a small distance before the others, had been attacked by a female bear with two cubs but another of [the men] arrived to his rescue, and shot her."

One of the richest lodes in the early literature on the bear was

opened in 1804 when President Thomas Jefferson sent Meriwether Lewis and William Clark to chart the way to the Pacific Ocean. The journals of Lewis and Clark and their associates are filled with hair-raising tales of encounters with "white" bears—a misnomer then in use by French traders and some Indians who were impressed by the silver tips of the grizzly's otherwise brownish hairs. According to Elliot Coues' edition of the journals, the first significant encounter occurred on April 29, 1805, somewhere on the Missouri River, beyond Fort Mandan:

"Captain Lewis, who was on shore with one hunter, met about eight o'clock two white bears. Of the strength and ferocity of this animal the Indians had given us dreadful accounts. They never attack him but in parties of six or eight persons, and even then are often defeated with a loss of one or more of their party. Having no weapons but bows and arrows, and the bad guns with which the traders supply them, they are obliged to approach very near to the bear; as no wound except through the head or heart is mortal, they frequently fall a sacrifice if they miss their aim. He rather attacks than avoids a man, and such is the terror he has inspired, that the Indians who go in quest of him paint themselves and perform all the superstitious rites customary when they make war on a neighboring nation.... On approaching these two, Captain Lewis and the hunter fired, and each wounded a bear. One of them made his escape; the other turned upon Captain Lewis and pursued him 70 or 80 yards, but being badly wounded the bear could not run so fast to prevent him from reloading his piece, which he again aimed at him, and a third shot from the hunter brought him to the ground."

On May 5 the party encountered another "white" bear. Sergeant Ordway wrote, "We shot him as he was swimming in the river." On May 11, William Bratton shot a grizzly through the lungs. The bear then chased Bratton for "a mile and a half." On May 14, near the Musselshell River, six men went out to kill a bear on a hillside. Wounded, the grizzly by Ordway's account "chased two of them into a canoe, and another into the river, and they steady firing at him. After shooting eight balls in his body ... [the bear] took the river and was near catching the man he chased in."

And on June 14, at the Great Falls of the Missouri, Lewis again was pursued by a grizzly that "ran open-mouthed and at full speed upon him." Lewis saved his skin by plunging into the river.

On the plains, it was fat and easy living for the great bear. Buffalo were plentiful. The vast herds were riddled with sick stragglers and each year offered up a new crop of vulnerable calves. Thousands of migrating buffalo drowned at the river crossings or were trampled in the wild scramble up and down the river-bottom bluffs. Like all bears, the grizzly was not so proud that it would turn up its nose at carrion. Yet in other plains matters, its pride was supreme. For want of a handy carcass or a stray calf, the bear would not hesitate to attack a grown buffalo bull, crushing the animal's hindquarters with the full impact of its awesome charge. Such habits honed the bear's arrogance to a fine edge. Of the plains grizzly, Lewis would write: "These bear being so hard to die rather intimidates us all. I must confess that I do not like the gentlemen and had rather fight two Indians than one bear."

Nearly all the roving explorers who followed Lewis' way west in the early 1800's corroborated his estimate of the bear's ferocity. There was, however, at least one dissenter. This was Zebulon Pike, who, returning from the southwestern mountains in 1807, presented President Jefferson with two grizzly cubs. In a letter to Jefferson the following year, Pike described how the cubs had followed "my men like dogs through our camps ... [playing] with each other and the soldiers." He begged Jefferson to assure some measure of humane care for the two captives (by then in the

CONTINUED ON PAGE 25

In 1833, Karl Bodmer depicted grizzlies
under attack on the upper Missouri River
in "Hunting of the Grizzly Bear." Artist
George Catlin, who preceded Bodmer up
the Missouri in 1831–32, had his own
encounter with the great beast: a gang of
bears broke into his camp one night and
chewed up his oil paints.

THE BEINECKE RARE BOOK AND MANUSCRIPT LIBRARY,
YALE UNIVERSITY, NEW HAVEN, CONN.

OVERLEAF: "People eat meat. Bears eat
meat. Some people eat bear meat," the
author notes—possibly including the
Indians in the undated painting
"Contested Game" by William Cary.

THE THOMAS GILCREASE INSTITUTE OF AMERICAN HISTORY
AND ART, TULSA, OKLA.

Wm de la Montagne Ca

A trapper gets his arm gnawed by a
California grizzly in this undated
primitive (probably from the 1850's). The
trapper is unidentified, but may well
have been mountain man Joe Meek, who
killed many bears—one of them, so the
legend goes, with a little hatchet.
BANCROFT LIBRARY, UNIVERSITY OF CALIFORNIA,
BERKELEY

PRECEDING PAGE: William R. Leigh's 1914
painting "A Close Call" was only a little
less gruesome than the anonymous
painting above.
THE THOMAS GILCREASE INSTITUTE OF AMERICAN HISTORY
AND ART, TULSA, OKLA.

custody of Philadelphia Museum curator Charles Willson Peale). And finally, as if to set the record straight as to the nature of the grizzly, he wrote, "they seldom or ever attack a man, unprovoked, but defend themselves courageously."

Pike's heroic vision of the bear apparently failed to attract many converts. Even trained scientists persisted in depicting the grizzly as a monster; and perhaps the most hyperbolic description came from none other than John Godman, the distinguished Pennsylvania naturalist. In Godman's view, the grizzly was "the despotic and sanguinary monarch of the wilds ... terrific in aspect ... ferociously bloodthirsty ... [causing] man himself to tremble at [its] approach. ..."

With the opening of the West to the fur trade, the grizzly's monarchy began to crumble. Now it was not just an occasional two-legged intruder to be chased ignominiously back into his canoe, but a seemingly endless flotilla of canoes and pirogues and keelboats, each bristling with fire sticks. Trappers in their wolfskin caps and fetid leathers had ample reason to fear the bear. And in their fear they despised it, and slew it with monotonous regularity. Unfortunately, so much of the record of this period has been distorted by Godmanesque exaggeration that it is difficult now to separate fact from fiction.

In the archives of my own family, for example, looms a larger-than-life fellow named Malcolm Clarke—a great-granduncle, I surmise by imperfect genealogical calculation, but a mountain man for certain. In 1841, Clarke hit out for the Upper Missouri with the American Fur Company. There he married a Piegan Blackfoot woman, one Cacocoma, sired four children, ranched a bit, and then of a summer evening in 1868 had the rotten luck to be gut-shot by his wife's own people. By then, Malcolm Clarke was something of a legend himself. The Piegans for a time had called him Four Bears, an honorary title and possibly an apocryphal one as well. One account has it that Clarke killed four grizzlies in a single morning, and all before breakfast. Another story holds that a huge bear once almost ended Clarke's career in a Montana huckleberry thicket. With a swipe or two of the paw, the bear is said to have lifted Clarke's scalp, knocked him down, worked him over for a moment on the ground, and then left him for dead. Whereupon a friendly Indian, passing by, spotted the dying trapper and with good-samaritan haste pasted the unhinged scalp back in place with spittle and chewing tobacco. So it is said, but I cannot vouch for it.

Far more implausible to me, though surer of documentation, is the saga of Hugh Glass, the doughty Scot who survived a terrible mauling at the forks of the Grand River in 1823. Old Hugh, an advance man for William H. Ashley's beaver trappers, apparently ran afoul of a she-grizzly out foraging with her cubs. By most accounts, it was combat at close range: Hugh with a long knife, the bear with five on each paw. Later, two companions (one, according to some chroniclers, being the young Jim Bridger) discovered Hugh's torn and lacerated body beneath the dead bear. The mountain man was still breathing. Figuring that Glass was too far gone to be moved, and with only a few hours of life left in him, the two trappers tended his wounds as best they could, dug a shallow grave nearby, and waited for the end. But Old Hugh refused to die. Finally, fearing for their own lives in such hostile country, the two bid a last farewell to their unconscious comrade and hurried away to catch up with the rest of the Ashley party. Soon thereafter, Glass regained his senses. Racked with fever and pain, he saw the open grave, realized he had been abandoned, and vowed to have revenge on the deserters. Thus motivated, the indomitable Scot proceeded to crawl a hundred miles on hands and knees, grubbing bugs and roots and the carrion remains of wolf-kills along the way, until he reached a tributary of the

Missouri. And from that point he floated by log the remaining 150 miles to Fort Kiowa. Eventually, Old Hugh confronted the two trappers, but the embers of his rage had cooled by then and he let them go. Perhaps it was enough for Hugh Glass that he had survived.

No doubt the Glass saga inspired less reliable tales of dread encounters betwen men and bears. In his classic volume *The Grizzly Bear*, William H. Wright concluded that much of the lore of the last century was sheer fiction. As Wright perceived it:

"[T]he old hunters and trappers, however well meaning they may be, are not to be relied upon for information that is worth much from a scientific standpoint. I well remember the first one I ever saw. He was an old, grizzled fellow, all covered with scars, which he claimed were the results of his encounters with grizzly bears, mountain lions and Indian arrows. ... He maintained that he had shot grizzlies that had gone a mile or more after receiving several mortal wounds, and that, when finally overtaken, they were found to have plugged up the bullet holes with moss to stop the flow of blood. ... [O]f course, we must not mix up the entirely distinct acts of lying and 'stuffing the tenderfoot.' When a man can neither read nor write, and lives most of his life alone on fresh venison and flapjacks, he is entitled to some amusement."

Still, dread encounters, however embellished in the telling, were common. Before the introduction of the breech-loading Sharps rifle in 1848, Western rovers were armed with muzzle-loaders. Even in the hands of a crack shot, these were pitifully inadequate tools to turn against a grizzly. The Kentucky long rifle carried by Lewis' men had an effective range of only seventy-five yards, and it took thirty seconds to reload. In that time, a charging grizzly could cover nearly three hundred yards. Consequently, as reconstructed by Andy Russell in his book *Grizzly Country*, "what started as a grizzly hunt often dissolved into a spirited foot race for the nearest tree." Russell further points out that a grizzly's heartbeat is relatively slow; that, as a result, the animal "takes a long time to bleed out even when struck in the heart." Thus, he adds, the hunter with a muzzle-loader, even after shooting a bear through the heart, sometimes was "desperately mauled or killed" a moment later.

If any Western state was ever grizzly country—and more than a few once were—it was California. Until the middle of the nineteenth century, bears by the thousands roamed the High Sierra and lesser mountains along the coast. The Los Angeles region, for example, swarmed with bears. Trapper Andrew Sublette tangled with one grizzly in a canyon behind what is now Santa Monica and later died of his wounds. And historian Horace Bell, reminiscing in 1881 on his earlier days as a back-country ranger, recalled that "grizzly bears were more plentiful in Southern California than pigs."

That the grizzly lasted as long as it did in California is something of a miracle, for nowhere else in its once wide domain was it pursued, baited, tortured, and slain with such unremitting human savagery. The Spanish *vaqueros* made a grim game of snaring a bear with their rawhide *reatas*, then dispatching the snarling animal with lances.

There were pit fights as well. Bears were roped, chained by the leg to a heavy post, and obliged to defend themselves against longhorn bulls. Quoting one account by an American journalist of the early 1800's, Horace Bell reported that bears and bulls were pitted against each other frequently at Pala, the outpost of Mission San Luís Rey near San Diego. In one bloody episode, the tethered bear rose on its hind legs to meet the assault of the first bull. When the horns were within a yard of the grizzly's breast, the bear seized the bull's head with both paws and "in a twinkling ... the bull lay limp as a rag, his neck broken." Three more bulls were sent against the bear. Two met the same fate as the first. The third gored the grizzly fatally. Bell also told of a grizzly sent in chains from Los Angeles to Monterrey, Mexico, where it was matched against "Parnell," a "man-killing African lion." According to Bell, the "great Californian handled the African king as a cat would a rat."

The California grizzly fared better with lions and bulls than with people; and with the discovery of gold in 1848 (and the introduction of the Sharps rifle), the grizzly's fate was sealed. In that signal year alone, five hunters delivered seven hundred grizzly pelts to Sutter's Fort at Sacramento. The pelts were stacked near the flagpole, at the top of which fluttered California's newly adopted flag—the flag of the golden bear.

The war between people and grizzly bears in North America has been largely a struggle for protein. People eat meat. Bears eat meat. Some people eat bear meat. The human appetite for bear flesh is probably as old as the flint-tipped spear. In more historic times, on the plains and in Old California, grizzlies were not simply dispatched for sport; more often than not their choice parts wound up in the assassin's stewpot. Osborne Russell, a member of Jim Bridger's Rocky Mountain Fur Company brigade, wrote of one such repast. "Our camp keeper," Russell noted, "had prepared an elegant supper of grizzly bear meat and mutton nicely stewed and seasoned with pepper and salt, which as the mountain phrase goes 'is not bad to take'!" In gold-rush California, grizzly meat was apparently considered a great delicacy. At the mining camp of El Dorado, hunters were paid $1.25 for a pound of it. Moreover, a slain bear yielded ancillary benefits. Wilderness prophet John Muir, who wandered the length and breadth of the High Sierra in the late 1800's, mentioned a few of them in his book *Our National Parks:*

" 'B'ar meat,' said a hunter from whom I was seeking information, 'b'ar meat is the best meat in the mountains; their skins make the best beds, and their grease the best butter. Biscuits shortened with b'ar grease goes as far as beans; a man will walk all day on a couple of them biscuit.' "

To what extent people have compensated the bear in kind is beyond statistical recall. Reports of bears devouring their human victims are extremely rare, even in the turgid buckskin fictions of the nineteenth century. People who have occasionally been close to the bear's jaws in adversary situations swear that the human odor seems to offend the animal—a condition that, if correct, might explain why few people attacked by grizzlies are killed on the spot, much less eaten.

Some old-timers insist that grizzlies once fed ravenously on sick and dying Indians in smallpox-ridden Western camps, thereby acquiring not only a taste for people meat but a tendency to stalk and devour healthy specimens as well. Possibly—yet to me it sounds as likely as Uncle Malcolm Clarke's scalp restorative in the huckleberry thicket. In recent years, nonetheless, there have been several instances in which grizzlies partly devoured their human prey. Such was the fate of Michele Koons, one of the two young women attacked and killed by separate grizzlies, in separate campsites only miles apart, at Glacier National Park in 1967. And in 1976, at Glacier Bay National Park in Alaska, searchers following grizzly tracks found the regurgitated remains of a missing backpacker. Incidents such as these awaken lingering human suspicions about the habits of grizzlies. In Montana, one wildlife official quoted a resident rancher as having proclaimed with conviction that the grizzly is "good for nuthin' [because it] sleeps all winter and eats people all summer."

Many Montana ranchers nowadays might take sharp issue with that assessment, insisting that the grizzly is good for *worse*

than nothing because, after sleeping all winter, it spends its summer eating cows. The introduction of livestock to grizzly country, beginning on a large scale in the 1860's, drastically accelerated the process of bear extirpation west of the Dakotas. With the bison going, going, gone, the great bear naturally turned to the next most plentiful and vulnerable ungulates to supplement its predominantly herbaceous diet. With prized longhorns and heifers and sheep becoming piles of fragmented bone overnight, the rancher just as naturally turned to cash bounties, poisons, posses, and set guns. And more tall grizzly tales: of "Old Mose," the Colorado stock-killer that reportedly did in five of its human pursuers; of "Two Toes" (the other three having been lost to a trap in Montana); and of "Old Ephraim," the elusive sheep-eater of northern Utah, pursued for thirteen years and finally shot by Frank Clark on August 22, 1923, in the Cache National Forest. In memory of Old Eph, the Cache County Boy Scouts later erected a monument. The inscription informs the mourner that Old Eph weighed 1,100 pounds and that his skull now resides in the custody of the Smithsonian Institution in Washington, D.C.

On August 1, 1975, under provisions of the Endangered Species Act, the U.S. Fish and Wildlife Service designated the grizzly bear in the coterminus United States a threatened species. One immediate effect of the ruling was the reinforcement of Montana's two-year-old moratorium on grizzly hunting. (Idaho has enforced a closed season since 1946; Wyoming, since 1972.) The federal-state regulations further stipulate that no more than twenty-five grizzlies may be "removed" from the Montana grizzly population in any one year—not only through sport hunting but for whatever reason, including the protection of persons and property and through accidental road-kills.

In recent years, however, sport hunting has not figured as prominently as it once did in the demise of the bear. From 1967 to 1975, the so-called "harvest" by trophy hunters in Montana averaged only nineteen bears a year. No doubt a heavier toll has been taken illegally by jack-lighting poachers and proxy hunters with assignments from trophy collectors in Texas, New York, and California, who reportedly have paid $3,000 for an adult grizzly hide, $500 for a full set of claws. Bear bladders are likewise in demand. At the time of the threatened species ruling in 1975, a West Coast clearinghouse was circulating handbills throughout western Montana, offering $50 per bladder, to be used "for a part of a new medicine." In fact, this new medicine was to be marketed in Japan as an aphrodisiac. "Please do not kill the bears for this reason only," the flyer piously suggested. "We would like to keep this business for a long time to come."

Wildlife officials remain deeply concerned about livestock grazing in the national forests of grizzly country. The real and imagined defense of cows and sheep still probably accounts for more dead bears than all other causes combined, excluding natural mortality. The Targhee National Forest, west of Yellowstone Park in Idaho, is prime sheep country. Stockmen there kill at least half a dozen grizzlies every year. East of Glacier National Park on the Blackfoot Reservation, cows help hold that tribe's fragile economy together. Not surprisingly, grizzlies are vermin in the eyes of the Blackfoot ranchers.

Logging operations also take a toll. Apologists claim that clear-cutting actually improves habitat, inasmuch as grizzlies prefer open country. While there may be some truth to this, it is doubtful grizzlies thrive when clear-cuts on high slopes result in soil slippage and erosion, as they most always do. Still, the real problem is not the manner of cutting trees, but of getting to them. Logging roads lace the forest lands of grizzly country. Montana Hunting Area 110, a section of the Flathead National Forest just

In Charlie Russell's "Bruin not Benny Turned the Leaders" (1924), the grizzly met Civilization and the grizzly won—for the moment. But the very presence of the stagecoach suggests that the long war between man and bear had entered its last chapter, for with the stagecoach came the miners, ranchers, and settlers, then the railroads, highways, national parks, and finally the tourists—who do not relish the dark presence of mortal danger in their wilderness.

west of Glacier Park and barely half its size, contains an estimated six hundred miles of logging roads, twice the aggregate of paved and unpaved roads within the park itself. Such roads provide easy access to hunters, licensed and unlicensed.

Then there is the problem of mineral and recreational development. Near Glacier Park, more than 200,000 acres of the Flathead Forest are under oil and gas lease applications. East of Yellowstone, the Sunlight and Needles Creek watersheds have been proposed for copper mining. West of Yellowstone, at Hebgen Lake, promoters are hustling plans for a huge ski resort and condominium complex. And north of Yellowstone is the burgeoning residential development at Big Sky. "You know what they're doing to us?" said a young ranger I met at Yellowstone Park. "They're closing the circle. One of these days the park will be all that's left. But it won't be enough for the grizzly."

Yellowstone and Glacier national parks already may not be enough for the bear. People are the problem. Historically, visitors have congregated in developed campgrounds, where they stepped on each other's feet and generated huge volumes of garbage. The garbage attracted the bears. The bears amused the people. Then the bears grew bolder and frightened the people. Some people were mauled. Rangers tracked down the culprits and transplanted them into the back country. But that didn't work; the bears came back. So some were "removed," either tranquilized and moved or shot dead. Next, scientists began to quibble about the parks' garbage dumps. The Craighead brothers, John and Frank, who had been studying grizzlies for years at Yellowstone, argued that the dumps should be phased out gradually. Glen Cole, the Park Service's chief biologist at Yellowstone, argued that the dumps should be closed pronto. Cold turkey for the grizzlies. Cole won the argument. There was much lingering acrimony—and many studies and investigations, which proved nothing, except that grizzlies and people do not mix congenially. Meanwhile, the bears were moving back into the more remote precincts of the park. But so were the people. In four years (1970-74), back-country use at Yellowstone Park increased 400 per cent as hikers and backpackers swarmed through the wilderness. Rangers were dispatched to the back country. Certain trails were closed. At Yellowstone, a young man backpacked into an area officially closed to hikers because of the known presence of grizzlies. A bear entered his campsite, sniffing food. The young man attempted to chase the bear away. The young man is dead. So it goes.

Such incidents as this, as well as the fatalities at Glacier in 1967 and in Alaska in 1976, have given rise to the idea that perhaps it would be best for all concerned, all *people* in any event, if grizzlies were eradicated from the two national parks; transplanted, if necessary, to some special refuge elsewhere, some open-air zoo where they would not interfere with people's enjoyment of Old Faithful or the Grinnell Glacier. Gairdner B. Moment, a Maryland gerontologist and visiting scientist at the National Institute of Health, offered just such a final solution in a series of articles appearing in the journal *BioScience* half a dozen years ago. Moment had been vacationing at Glacier National Park at the time the two young women were killed by bears, and apparently he was deeply moved by the episode. "I can find no directive in the Ten Commandments or even in the New Morality of situation ethics," he wrote, "requiring that every species be saved from extinction." Moment then delivered his manifesto:

"Every park cannot serve every purpose under the sun, no matter how worthy.... Old Faithful and St. Mary Lake [at Glacier] cannot be seen elsewhere nor can they be transplanted. Grizzlies can.... If we are as anxious to see grizzlies as we evidently are to shoot ducks, grizzlies could be established in Wildlife Refuges outside of parks. In those locations, grizzlies could provide the danger some people seek...."

Despite the fact that grizzlies are little more transplantable than geysers, Moment's grim proposal bears watching. Total removal of grizzlies from the parks is always a possibility. We Americans are passionately devoted to personal safety. We absolutely insist on it. Given the worst combination of circumstances—a quadrupling of back-country pressures, a series of maulings, perhaps a repeat performance of Glacier's haunting "Night of the Grizzly"—it could happen. Then—good-by, bears. The war is finally over. We win? No, I think not. We lose.

John G. Mitchell, former editor in chief of Sierra Club Books and current field editor for Audubon *magazine, is the author of* Losing Ground *(Sierra Club Books, 1974).*

OPPOSITE: PHOTO BY PERRY SHANKLE, JR.

SOLVING THE ENERGY CRISIS

Long before the energy crunch became a crisis, Rube Goldberg was lampooning the American fascination with gadgetry that helped bring it about. His first invention—an "automatic weight reducing machine" that employed a doughnut, a bomb, a balloon, a hot stove, and a giant bell to strip pounds from a fat man— appeared in the New York Evening Mail *in 1914. Thereafter, until his death in 1970, Goldberg was a national favorite, and his name became synonymous with any complicated device intended to perform a simple task. Goldberg once explained that the inspiration for his inventions— and for their inventor, Professor Lucifer G. Butts—came from college chemistry classes: "You know how the professor stands up behind a long table . . . with a lot of retorts and test tubes and bottles and lamps . . . all strung out in front of him, and starts at one end to demonstrate something and winds up at the other end with the absolute proof that something or other has one per cent of sodium in it." No matter how convoluted his schemes, Professor Butts bent every effort to minimize the energy expended.*

THE PROFESSOR TURNS ON HIS THINK-FAUCET AND DOPES OUT A MACHINE FOR WASHING DISHES WHILE YOU ARE AT THE MOVIES. WHEN SPOILED TOMCAT (A) DISCOVERS HE IS ALONE HE LETS OUT A YELL WHICH SCARES MOUSE (B) INTO JUMPING INTO BASKET (C), CAUSING LEVER END (D) TO RISE AND PULL STRING (E) WHICH SNAPS AUTOMATIC CIGAR-LIGHTER (F). FLAME (G) STARTS FIRE SPRINKLER (H). WATER RUNS ON DISHES (I) AND DRIPS INTO SINK (J). TURTLE (K), THINKING HE HEARS BABBLING BROOK BABBLING, AND HAVING NO SENSE OF DIRECTION, STARTS WRONG WAY AND PULLS STRING (L), WHICH TURNS ON SWITCH (M) THAT STARTS ELECTRIC GLOW HEATER (N). HEAT RAY (O) DRIES THE DISHES.

IF THE CAT AND THE TURTLE GET ON TO YOUR SCHEME AND REFUSE TO COOPERATE, SIMPLY PUT THE DISHES ON THE FRONT PORCH AND PRAY FOR RAIN.

Butts and his creator are gone now, just when we need them most. But, as shown by the seriously patented inventions on the following two pages, real-life tinkerers were at work on the problem before Goldberg came on the scene. We offer their ideas as our contribution to the energy debate; perhaps their time has come at last.

"Professor Butts's Automatic Dishwasher," by Rube Goldberg

An ingenious 1870 solution for those who today are unable or unwilling to give up the family car: a pair of pets provide the power; not a drop of gas is guzzled.

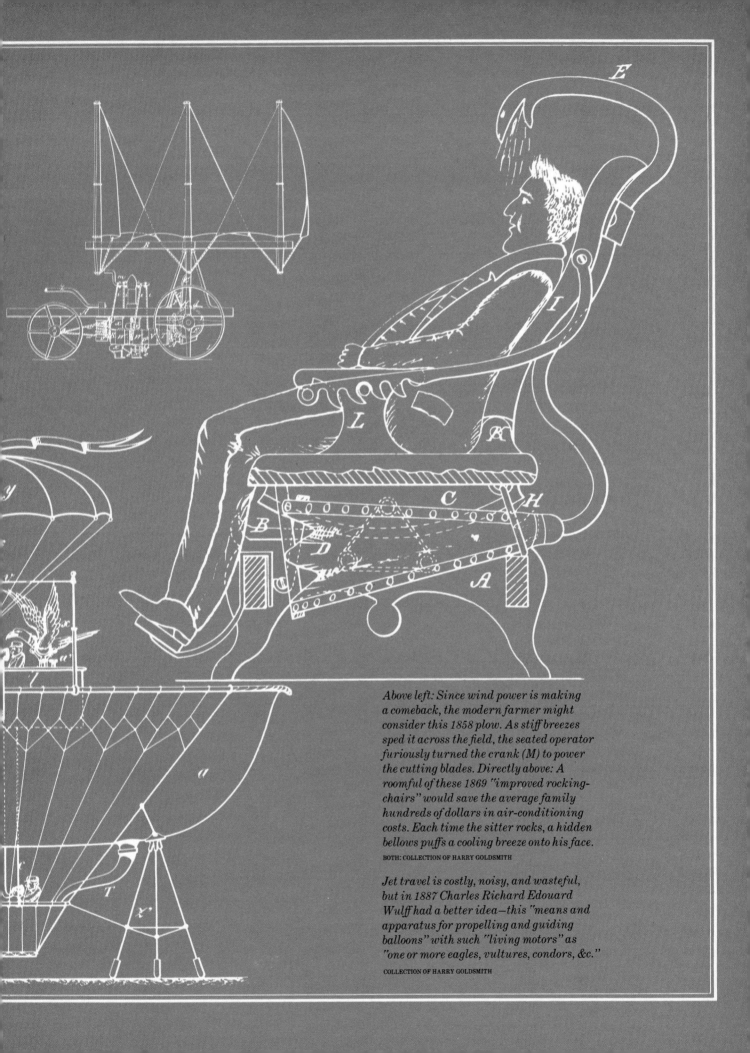

Above left: Since wind power is making a comeback, the modern farmer might consider this 1858 plow. As stiff breezes sped it across the field, the seated operator furiously turned the crank (M) to power the cutting blades. Directly above: A roomful of these 1869 "improved rocking-chairs" would save the average family hundreds of dollars in air-conditioning costs. Each time the sitter rocks, a hidden bellows puffs a cooling breeze onto his face.
BOTH: COLLECTION OF HARRY GOLDSMITH

Jet travel is costly, noisy, and wasteful, but in 1887 Charles Richard Edouard Wulff had a better idea—this "means and apparatus for propelling and guiding balloons" with such "living motors" as "one or more eagles, vultures, condors, &c."

COLLECTION OF HARRY GOLDSMITH

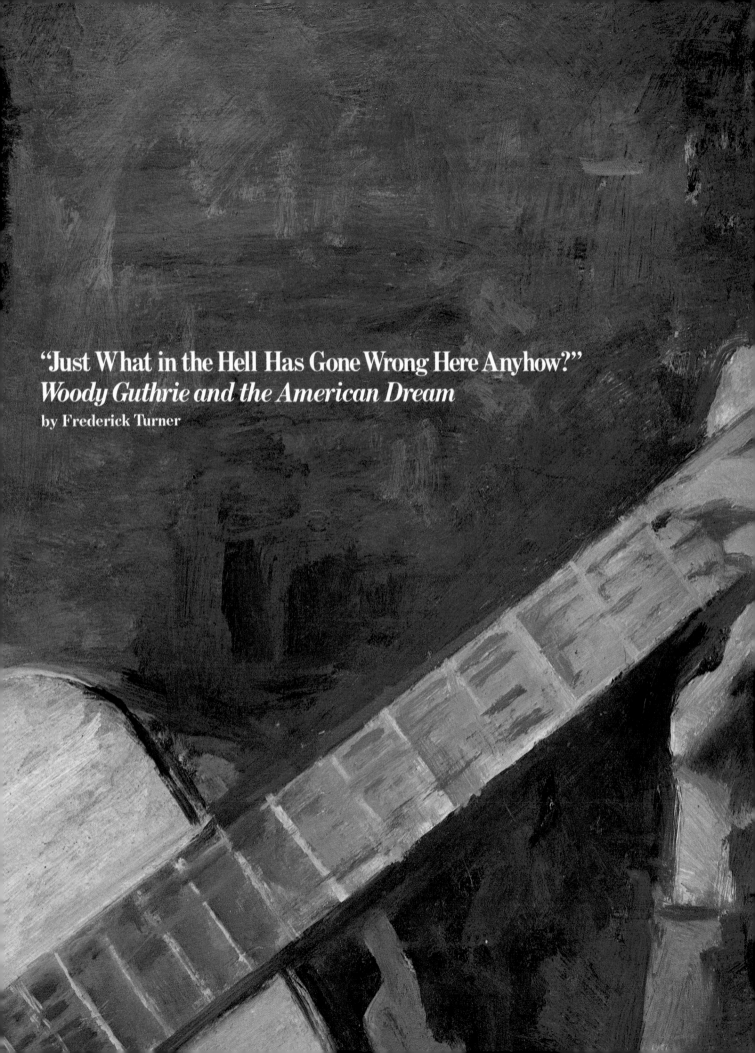

"Just What in the Hell Has Gone Wrong Here Anyhow?"
Woody Guthrie and the American Dream
by Frederick Turner

We seem to be in the midst of a Woody Guthrie boom. Its crest was the 1976 film *Bound for Glory*, which attracted considerable critical attention before it went out into shopping center cinemas across the land. Two collections of Guthrie's fugitive writings are now in circulation, and there is a handsome, spanking new *Woody Guthrie Songbook*, as well as two mass market editions of the autobiographical work on which the film was based and the first publication of a work he wrote more than thirty years ago, *Seeds of Man*. Record bins are amply stocked with "—— Sings Woody Guthrie," and with reissues of his own recordings long unavailable.

The subject of this boom was a tough, troubled, weedy little man with survival instincts as strong as the iron grass and mesquite of his native Oklahoma and Texas. He was born in Okemah, Oklahoma, in 1912 into what passed then and there for middle-class circumstances, but he grew up in an atmosphere of familial misfortune and disintegration tallying that of the region as a whole. In his teens he followed his father down to the high plains of Texas and there began a career as a wandering minstrel that took him through most of the states of the Union, hundreds of bars, halls, recording studios, street corners, hobo camps, wartime troopships. As Guthrie summarized it in the early forties:

"[I] sung along the boweries of forty-two states; Reno Avenue in Oklahoma City, Lower Pike Street in Seattle, the jury table in Santa Fe; the Hooversvilles on the flea-bit rims of your city's garbage dump. I sung in the camps called 'Little Mexico,' on the dirty edge of California's green pastures. I sung on the gravel barges of the East Coast and along New York's Bowery watching the cops chase the bay-rum drinkers. I curved along the bend of the Gulf of Mexico and sung with the tars and salts in Port Arthur, the oilers and greasers in Texas City, the marijuana smokers in the flop town in Houston. I trailed the fairs and rodeos all over Northern California, Grass Valley, Nevada City; I trailed the apricots and peaches around Marysville. . . . Everywhere I went I throwed my hat down in the floor and sung for my tips."

The road ended in hospitals, where he spent almost all of his last fifteen years gripped in the twisted fingers of the incurable, hereditary Huntington's Disease. When he died in 1967 he was legendary among the performers and consumers who made up the "folk movement" of the sixties. In those last years of enforced silence and involuntary muscular activity,

through the long days of waiting, a trickle of visitors came to his bedside: the three children of his last family, led by his second wife, Marjorie; admiring performers like Pete Seeger and Bob Dylan; professional writers and folklorists. And out of that medicinal room, in that time of a new radicalism, Woody Guthrie was made into a symbol of folk protest as he had once himself sought to be in the proletarian thirties and early forties.

That he is now the fit subject of popularization on a far wider scale suggests, among other things, that the political stink of radicalism no longer clings to his name, and that the process of time that transforms all radicals into patriots and all revolutions into glorious blows for human liberty has been at work here.

Few know and fewer care now that Guthrie wrote some communistic journalism, that he came to accept the notion that America was in the clutches of a Wall Street-inspired conspiracy against working people, or that he looked forward to the total reorganization of American society as it was then (and now) and to the birth of a new socialistic one out of it.

They are right not to care about Guthrie's engagement in formal politics: he was so bad a politician, so hopelessly naive, so radically individual, that even the Communist party wouldn't have him—though he would have had them. In his better moments he knew this, too: "I just think how I think is right and let you do the same. I don't care what party believes it or any part of it. I didn't never want to be no politician, they's too many crooked ones without me."

And so what remains is the perdurable Guthrie, the person beyond politics and political uses. This is the quintessentially American Woody Guthrie who was almost mystically endowed with a profound understanding of the spirit of this land and whose life and work expressed a fierce and steady devotion to America's promise as a nation founded on the belief in the dignity and divinity of each of us.

To see Guthrie in this way—culturally rather than merely politically—is to see him as an archetypal American who embodied much of our common history with all its troubles and thwarted excellences. And seeing him this way we can also see that he belongs to one of our most honorable traditions: those artists who have taken America seriously. I mean those whose lines and syllables are public acts insisting upon the very best from us, "necessary affirmations" (as the Chilean poet Pablo Neruda called them) of the worth and dignity of all persons and of this country as uniquely fitted to allow their

expression. Emerson, Thoreau, Whitman, and William Carlos Williams come first to mind here, and Woody Guthrie takes his place among them as easily and naturally as the colors, smells, and rhythms of our common life once sprang from his lips and fingers.

Guthrie knew all about booms. He knew firsthand their terrible ephemerality, for he had seen his home town of Okemah stretch and collapse like an accordion in an oil boom at the beginning of the twenties.

Long before, this had been the roaming territory of the Wichita and Comanche tribes. Later it became part of the dumping ground for tribes dispossessed elsewhere. And still later it was a part of the Creek reservation until at last it fell into white hands. "Okemah" in Creek means "town on a hill," and a rail junction established there in the first years of this century put a small dot on the region's map.

Guthrie's family was much like the rest—whites pouring into newly opened territory, southward out of Kansas, northward out of Texas. His maternal grandmother had been a log cabin schoolteacher when what became Okfuskee County was still Indian Territory. His father, Charlie, had been a cowboy and then a store clerk in Bell County, Texas. In Oklahoma he branched out into real-estate speculation, stockbreeding, and politics, while his wife Nora was giving him five children. If fortune had been otherwise, it is possible that the Guthries would be regarded today as one of the state's founding families.

Woodrow Wilson Guthrie was the third of those five children, raised in his earliest years amidst the trappings of his father's hectic and precarious success in a town small enough that "on your way to the post office, you'd nod and speak to so many friends that your neck would be rubbed raw."

There was a minor key here, though, the sound of a sadness that coursed through the noise of the family's expanding prosperity. It was in his mother, in her voice, in those old tragic ballads she sang out of her Scotch-Irish background. It was as if even in its brief days of happiness the doom and dissolution of the family were prefigured in these sung narratives of love and love's end; just as in the high boom days about to come to the town the sure signs of collapse could have been read.

One day the family's pleasant seven-room house burned to the ground and they all heard in the stillness that minor key. They had to move to the tail end of town to an older house, the dank walls of which reflected the change. And there was more of the same to come, swiftly now, as though something had been loosed that could never again be brought together. Like a runner badly bumped off stride Charlie Guthrie scrambled madly to keep his balance, all the while falling farther behind. There was a cyclone that tore this older house to pieces. And then the death by fire of Woody's older sister, Clara. And bad land gambles that quickly dissipated all of Charlie's holdings. And finally the oil boom that instantly transformed Okemah into a jungle of main-chancers in yet another microcosmic recapitulation of our frontier heritage.

First there came the rig builders, Guthrie wrote, "cement men, carpenters, teamskinners, wild tribes of horse traders and gypsy wagons loaded full, and the wheels breaking down; crooked gamblers, pimps, whores, dope fiends, and peddlers, stray musicians and street singers, preachers cussing about love and begging for tips on the street corners, Indians in dirty loud clothes chanting along the sidewalks with their kids crawling and playing in the filth and grime underfoot. People elbowed up and down the streets like a flood on the Canadian, and us kids would run and jump right in the big middle of the crowds, and let them sort of push us along a block or so, and play like we was floating down stream. Thousands of folks come to town to work, eat, sleep, celebrate, pray, cry, sing, talk, argue, and fight with the older settlers." The town's population exploded from a couple of thousand to fifteen thousand and the smell and taste of oil and fast money filled the air.

But through it all, the Guthries did not prosper. The sadness in Nora Guthrie had by now manifested itself in acts of terrible, random destructiveness, flinging crockery and furniture against the walls, moaning, frothing at the mouth. The children cowered in the corners, unwitting witnesses to the power of that same Huntington's Disease that would one day take the small boy who watched now. Later he wrote: "I hate a hundred times more to describe my own mother in any such words as these. You hate to read about a mother described in any such words as these. I know. I understand you. I hope you can understand me, for it must be broke down and said." When she had calmed again, the children would pick up the pieces and straighten the rooms so that when Charlie Guthrie dragged himself home at evening after another defeated day in the boom race things would look almost normal.

In 1923 in the midst of the boom the family had to admit defeat. Charlie had lost it all by now and could not even pay the

rent on their house. They moved out to Oklahoma City, and when they returned to Okemah a year later the boom was over and the town had settled back to tough it out as a tiny way station in the midst of chronic depression.

They took up life here again with those others stranded in the now shriveled "town on a hill" with the wind rising and the sandy soil beginning to swirl about the abandoned oil works and the survivor sumac and cottonwood and the dry, beaten pastures. Charlie caught part of another boom, belatedly come to these rural Southwestern stretches. Now he sold auto license tags for the state, and for a moment things looked up. But then again: home fire, this time even more catastrophic. Guthrie hinted in *Bound for Glory* that his mother may have involuntarily set it. However it happened, Charlie Guthrie was terribly blistered in trying to put it out, and when the last had been extinguished, Nora Guthrie was well on her train-bound way to the state asylum at Norman on a one-way ticket.

Charlie went to convalesce with a sister in Texas while Woody, now thirteen, and his older brother Roy stayed on in Okemah. Mostly Woody lived by himself for two years in various abandoned buildings. In a hand-to-mouth existence he picked up junk and sold it to buy his meals. In those summers of 1928 and 1929 he hit roads out of town for what work he could find, hoeing figs, picking grapes, working his way as far south as the wharfed and furbelowed town of Galveston. Now in these hot days he carried a harmonica on his travels and sang the old ballads Nora had once sung while he brushed her hair in the precious calm. And he began also to pick up other songs, the songs of traveling, working, hard-luck America: blues, jig tunes, Indian shouts, truck driver company-keepers.

At the end of the summer of 1929 he decided to join his father again in another oil boom town, Pampa, Texas. Behind him he left apparently little besides the faded, almost anonymous entry in *The Creekehoma*, the high-school yearbook. Beneath a somber, too-old face, a white shirt and bow tie, the legend: "Woodrow Guthrie, Panther Staff '28, Publication Club '29, Glee Club '29."

Standing on Okemah's Main Street in an early morning haze with a hot Southwestern sun still in the offing across the flats below, it is easy to see this town as it was before the boom and after. There is still life here, and one could watch Okemah waking to its hard and homely tasks much like many another town west of the Mississippi, the gaggle of pick-ups parked at the

Music was Woody's passport from the time he left his home in Okemah, Oklahoma (top), through two years of high school (center—he is in the middle), and on to Pampa, Texas, where he organized a country-western group (bottom—Woody is at the far left in the unlikely moustache).

PAGES 34–35: OIL PAINTING OF WOODY GUTHRIE BY JOSH MACRAE. COLLECTION OF MARJORIE GUTHRIE. THIS PAGE, ALL: COLLECTION OF MARJORIE GUTHRIE.

"I knew that my trail would be a story that whirls, and a song that spins in the middle of the sun, a hunt for the universe on the points of our needles. I knew the tale would be a freewheeler, a quick starter, but a high running, circling chorus that keeps on repeating over and over, and would sing every song to be sung. . . ."

FROM *American Folksong.* COPYRIGHT © 1947 BY FOLKWAYS RECORDS, REPRINTED BY SPECIAL PERMISSION OF MOSES ASCH.

Top: In Pampa, Woody married a "fine Irish girl" named Mary Jennings and fathered three children; the family is seen here about 1938. Bottom: Woody hits the road in 1939.

COLLECTION OF MARJORIE GUTHRIE

*"I've been having some hard traveling,
    I thought you knowed,
I've been having some hard traveling,
    way down the road,
I've been doing some hard rambling,
    hard drinking, hard gambling,
I've been hitting some hard
    traveling, Lord."*

preferred breakfast spot, a few figures paused on sidewalks to read newspaper headlines, and a bunch of kids with towels and swim suits gathering outside the YMCA. Only a water tower above the flat roofs confers singularity on Okemah, for it announces that this was the "Home of Woody Guthrie."

Indeed it was. And despite the fact that Guthrie left here even before finishing high school, he never ceased to regard it as home. Yet out here far from the media blitz, the record stores and book shops, there is still some genuine hostility to the poet. They have not entirely forgotten his subsequent leftist activities, and the sign on the water tower was put up there only over opposition. For the losers in this local skirmish Guthrie was "no good," a trouble-maker, a Communist, so the sight of the water tower must be a daily offense.

Guthrie often admitted that he and trouble traveled together, but almost as often he insisted that he didn't cause the troubles he sang about but merely called attention to them. As he once wrote of crickets:

"Crickets don't eat houses down. Crickets just hang around to sing that the damn thing's a falling down. He'll be there a long time singing about it. . . .

"Then the other bugs that really brought the house down will run off somewhere and they'll say, Look at that god damn cricket, he was there all of th' time! He's th' one! Get 'im! He lives in rot an' filth all of th' time! He causes it! He believes in it! He spreads it around! Get that bastardly son of a bitch! And the cricket don't want to live nowheres else. He had to stay on the job and holler and sing that the house was rotting down. He had to stay."

So there is this ambivalent situation here: the artist's love of a place he left early and that place's mingled pride and anger that he was ever there at all. There is a gravestone for him in the local cemetery, but the clay beneath it is empty. Guthrie's ashes were scattered over other lands and waters. And there is the house on the southern fringe of town where the Guthrie family once lived until driven out by the cyclone. Some years ago a local businessman purchased it to turn it into a memorial of some kind. An amiable gent I asked for directions to it seemed innocent of any resentment toward another of the Guthrie pilgrims who stops here on the way to somewhere else.

But the house itself reinforces the local ambivalence: it is a crumbling, rotting wreck, all but hidden even on its hilltop by grasses, tangled creepers, fallen tree trunks. Its mold-green roof sags earthward, its porch from which the boy looked out on all there was to see of Oklahoma is gone, and the east wall is braced by poles that are losing the slow battle. As Marjorie Guthrie told me, the family and friends remain undecided as to what to do with it, and the cause of their indecision is the community hostility. Pete Seeger wants to turn it into a sort of way station for wandering young people. But, she said, her son Arlo, young enough to have a different sense of things, feels this probably would not work because of local attitudes toward "hippies."

So here it sits and settles. Inside, its shaky rooms smell of stale urine, and they are littered with the random, cast-away evidence that, memorial or no, this is a youth hang-out. Slogans on the ruined, peeling walls are about equally divided between allegiance to the symbol of Guthrie and to male pubescent fantasies of the flesh. From the high east windows you can gaze past vines and leaves down onto the flats that are dotted with agricultural outbuildings and the bobbing, hobbyhorse shapes of oil derricks.

On the land just back of the house Russell Bradley lives surrounded by his neat vegetable patch on which he raises "abundant crops." We talked some through the vines of his pole beans, and he mentioned the occasional inconvenience of living next to the old homestead.

"Some that comes here respects me and some don't," he said. "Why, there was a bunch through here Sunday: tromped all over my tomaters."

But there is no resentment of Guthrie himself. "Hell," said Bradley, "I lived through that Depression. If I'd a had a guitar and could sing, I'd a done anything for a quarter."

On the high Texas plains, Guthrie and the shattered remnants of his family became indistinguishable from the other Dust Bowl refugees who now began to drift before the winds, the dust storms, and the general economic blight that had overspread the nation.

The young man, his father, and his uncle Jeff tried one thing after another—clerking, police work, prospecting—in attempts to sink roots deep enough to withstand this weather. They failed, and it might be said that Okemah was the last and only home Woody Guthrie ever had, miserable and tragic as it so often was. For the rest of his life he was a wanderer, by necessity and by vocational choice. For here in Texas Guthrie discovered his career as a hard-traveling troubador.

From his uncle he learned to play guitar, and together they began to play country dances, rodeos, and carnivals. They sang for a while on a tiny, low-watt radio station. But Guthrie was different from the other busking singers and players who answered the modest needs of these hard-hit people. He was different because he saw in their straitened, often pathetic, lives, in these least little entertainments they could allow themselves, his own calling. It amounted to nothing less than a religious conviction that he was meant to sing these people's story, to sing to them, and to follow them wherever they went. More than this, the young man sensed that in these people lay the paradoxical essence of this country: this vast land with its mute, geophysical promises of freedom, equality, and plenty, its historic commitment to these same, and the dispossessed workers who stumbled and drifted about over its surfaces in search of the fulfillment of these promises. Somehow, in a way that must always elude accurate description, the spirit of the land and the plight of the common people entered into Guthrie and consumed him. It made him restless, cantankerous, moody, impossible to live with. It also made him inexhaustibly generous of himself, and it gave an unimpeachable power and authenticity to his art.

Unlearned in any formal sense, Guthrie before attaining his majority had mastered his lands and times in a deep, intuitive way. During the great intellectual ferment a century before the Dust Bowl, Emerson and Thoreau had noted the critical national need for such knowledge of America and for voices that could sing it. In the prim environs of Concord these men had divined a hollowness of heart beneath the often hysterical pretensions to national greatness, a hollowness that bespoke the unrealized ideals of the land and its people. Both thought that only someone with the imaginative power to incorporate the national history and make it his own could successfully articulate the problem and in doing so remind Americans of what this country was truly meant to be. Thoreau had tried this in *Walden.* Emerson guessed it might have to be the work of some unknown folk singer whose roots were sunk in the common soil.

Spare and straight and with still a whisper of Puritanism about him, Emerson had a courageous and daring imagination. In "The Poet" he dared to imagine a singer so close to the primitive that his language would bud from the earth in natural images, a singer with heart and genitals as well as head and brain. The picture language of this singer would be a song of freedom, of the inviolable sanctity of the individual conscience, and of the divinity within. America was itself the greatest poem, as yet unsung because these promises were as yet unrealized.

The singer as Emerson imagined him was thus both articulator of the national myth and a subversive, both sponsor of the culture and antagonist of it; in either role, he would be beyond mere patriotism. As he would sing the promise of America he would remind Americans unpleasantly of national deceits and shams, of the shabby political betrayals of the great myth, of the great land that had given birth to it.

Emerson was, of course, far in advance of his time—and still may be of ours—and when he dared to speak of the divine spark within each person, the Harvard Divinity School excused him for nearly thirty years from further guest appearances.

Whitman also was too far ahead—in part because he had read his Emerson and taken it much to heart. He was so much what the master had imagined, with his freedom-bent lines, his incorporation of geography, his unabashed physicality, that at first Emerson tried to tone down this powerhouse singer out of nowhere and then dissociated himself from Whitman forever. For despite Whitman's flag-waving, Fourth-of-July rhetoric, he really *was* that subversive myth-maker Emerson had called for. His songs were acts in history, his vision one that spoke of old dreams conveniently forgotten in the broad rush of expansionist America, dreams drowned by the roar of finance capitalism, railroads, steam whistles.

"This," Whitman wrote, "is what you shall do: Love the earth and the sun and animals, despise riches, give alms to every one that asks, stand up for the stupid and crazy, devote your income and labor to others, hate tyrants, argue not concerning God, have patience and indulgence toward the people, take off your hat to nothing known or unknown or to any man or numbers of men, go freely with powerful uneducated persons and with the young and with the mothers of families ... dismiss whatever insults your own soul, and your very flesh shall be a great poem."

This is Guthrie to a dot. And clearly there is much in this program that went against the American grain as it had developed. Which is probably why Whitman never found such a kindred artistic soul in his own lifetime, and after a couple of decades of looking for a Woody Guthrie, he had to admit it:

"I say I have not seen a single writer, artist, lecturer, or what not, that has confronted the voiceless but ever erect and active, pervading, underlying will and typic aspiration of the land, in a spirit kindred to itself. Do you call these genteel little creatures American poets? Do you term that perpetual, pistareen, paste-pot work American art . . . ? I think I hear, echoed as from some mountain-top afar in the west, the scornful laugh of the Genius of these States."

I do not know just how much of this great predecessor Guthrie read, but his identification with the voiceless poor, his unwearied insistence upon the myth of America, clearly predates knowledge of Whitman and goes deeper than any book. "Books," he once observed, "is all right. Far as books go, but as far as they go, they still don't go far enough." If we can trust his two autobiographical works, *Bound for Glory* and *Seeds of Man* ("lifebound novels," he called them, "both real and unreal"), Guthrie became like Whitman a subversive myth-speaker because he had witnessed the greatness of heart of American people in travail, deprivation, and bewilderment. And he saw these people in a huge, fecund landscape that still beckoned with dreams of dignity, justice, and plenitude.

He watched the beginnings of the Dust Bowl, first in Okemah and then in Texas, the uprooting of families, the collapse of farms. And on a prospecting trip into the Big Bend wilderness on the Texas-Mexico border he encountered endemic poverty that would outlast any dust storm. Here he saw again and anew the land, various, rich even in these spiky, rocky defiles and bottoms, and the people who somehow could not lay their hands on the naked necessities. He heard death underneath the unmuffled roar of trucks carting wetbacks to stoop labor and saw terror in the eyes of parentless children. He heard also the inexhaustible beauty of the human spirit in the music of the people's stray, casual talk and laughter. He learned, also, of the folly of ownership of land and that his own lust for the riches of a lost silver mine was surely the curse that had blighted the myth he was then learning and that he would subsequently sing. As he remembered it later:

"And there on the Texas plains right in the center of the dust bowl, with the oil boom over and the wheat blowed out and the hard-working people just stumbling about, bothered with mortgages, debts, bills, sickness, worries of every blowing kind, I seen there was plenty to make up songs about. . . .

"I never did make up many songs about the cow trails or the moon skipping through the sky, but at first it was funny songs of what all's wrong, and how it turned out good or bad. Then I got a little braver and made up songs telling what I

thought was wrong and how to make it right, songs that said what everybody in that country was thinking. And this has held me ever since."

This did hold him, a spellbound captive, and he held to it until the early fifties, after which he was unable to hold to anything. It was indeed the one great love of his life, transcending wives, children, friends, all the natural comforts of home, security, a steady job, lucrative recording contracts.

Perhaps only Marjorie Guthrie, his second wife and the one who cared for him all through those last years, really understood this. Speaking of that first wife Guthrie had married in Pampa and later left behind, she told me, "I'm sure if I'd been the one left behind out there, I wouldn't have understood. As a young mother, I'm sure I wouldn't have known why Woody *had* to travel. But when we met [in 1940 in New York] I was older, and since I had a creative life of my own, I could understand his. I always thought of him as going *to* something rather than *away* from something."

But undoubtedly it was very hard to understand this driven man, and she remembered once trying to console one of the daughters of that Texas marriage. Sitting in the dark on the edge of the girl's bed, Marjorie had told her that even if Woody wasn't a very good father to her, he was a very important person. Important because he was trying to make America a better place for *all* children. If this sounds sophistical to us, it may be because we cannot take Guthrie's commitment as seriously as he did; and it might even mean that we do not take the American promise as seriously as he did.

Forty years ago Guthrie hit the "long lonesome" out of the Texas Dust Bowl for what he and the other refugees mockingly referred to as the "ole Peach Bowl," California's "Garden of Eden." Behind him he left his young wife Mary and their two girls, Gwendellyn Gail and Sue. Like a great many other men of that time his plan was to find work and make enough money to send for the family—though surely other needs were mixed in here as well.

The experience of migration was an impressive one, tallying with those he had had as a drifter and down-and-outer in Okemah, Pampa, and the Big Bend country. Here again on the farthest coast was the American paradox: border patrols as if these American refugees were aliens; fruit and vegetables rotting on the ground or dumped in refuse pits, rather than given to the hungry; jungle camps growing typhoid, desperation, and debt;

Woody in New York, killing the fascists with song—clockwise from upper left: his first New York appearance, about 1939; with his second wife, Marjorie Mazia, 1945; belting out a song with Lee Hayes, Burl Ives, and Cisco Houston, 1945; serenading servicemen during the war; as the Pied Piper of the lower West Side; singing in McSorley's Old Ale House; in an evocative portrait, about 1943; relaxing with fellow troubador Burl Ives in Central Park, 1940.

"I walked along, the day just leaving out over the tops of the tall buildings, and sifting through the old scarred chimneys sticking up. Thank the good Lord, everybody, everything ain't all slicked up, and starched and imitation. Thank God, everybody ain't afraid. Afraid in the skyscrapers, and afraid in the red tape offices, and afraid in the tick of the little machine that never explodes, stock market tickers, that scare how many to death, ticking off deaths, marriages and divorces, friends and enemies. . . ."

and at the same time radio stations and newspapers willing to pay good money to someone who could describe all this. And Guthrie could, beginning with an outraged question, "Just what in the hell has gone wrong here anyhow?" but then passing on to songs where the love and the promise are bitterly juxtaposed with the impoverished realities just as the workers themselves were juxtaposed with the green fertility of the land and the unattainable alabaster sectors of the cities.

There were more than 200,000 refugees in the state in the last years of the thirties, and so there was a market of sorts for artists who could sing and play their music. Guthrie got a job singing on KFVD in Los Angeles and then sent for Mary and the girls. A third child, Bill Rogers, was born to them out there.

By then, Guthrie was on the road again: he spent most of his time in California singing for the migrants in their jungle camps, in the federal work camps, and helping to organize cannery and factory workers. Here began his association with the Communist party. He sang for the party, wrote columns for party publications, and espoused party programs over the air. It is a measure of the times that his fame as a singer dates from precisely this period, and while on KFVD he received more than twenty thousand letters in two years, many of them with crumpled bills in them to help keep him on the air. At some point he apparently tried officially to join the party but was rejected. Perhaps party bureaucrats saw that no political structure could ever hope to contain this natural force. Thereafter, though his solutions to social ills remained radical, Guthrie was entirely free of identification with any specific political movement.

Like all folk geniuses (and many a formally trained one as well) Guthrie was a profligate artist. At his best he is incomparable and elsewhere best ignored. But out of this period of the late thirties and on through the following decade he produced a remarkable body of song, both musical and written. Ballads of the Dust Bowl and songs of the refugees: "Talking Dust Bowl," "Dust Storm Disaster," "Pretty Boy Floyd," "So Long It's Been Good To Know Yuh," "Do Re Mi," "Going Down This Road," "Deportee." Songs of work like the twenty-six he spun while watching the Grand Coulee Dam project get started. Songs of play like his delightful children's songs. And the Joad ballads drawn from Steinbeck's *Grapes of Wrath* ("Rapes of Graft," as Guthrie had it). Plus the two large autobiographical books.

By the time he had completed *Seeds of Man* he was as acclimated to New York as he would ever be. He had gone there in 1940 in response to a letter from an actor friend of California days, Will Geer, who was playing on Broadway in *Tobacco Road*. The letter said there was more work and more action in New York, and so once again he left Mary and the children behind, this time with her family in Texas. Within a year Guthrie had divorced her and married Marjorie Mazia, a dancer with Martha Graham. These two small, intense people remained connected, especially in spirit, until the end of Guthrie's life.

At first they shared a room so tiny that when the bed was unfolded there was no unoccupied space. Except in one corner. There where the walls made an "L" was a triangular desk with bulletin-board material above it. And there the troubador wrote. At night when Marjorie returned home from teaching dance they would take turns reading to each other the reams that he had spun out of the deprivations of the past, the inequities of the present.

Through such writings but more through his singing and recordings Guthrie now became an important part of that odd but vital New York subculture of folk musicians that included at one time or another Pete Seeger, Burl Ives, Josh White, Leadbelly, Sonny Terry and Brownie McGhee, Millard Lampell, Lee Hays, and Jean Ritchie. Alan Lomax affixed the stamp of official recognition on him through extensive recordings for the Library of Congress, and Victor released his album of Dust Bowl ballads. The sound Guthrie got into these records was that of the high winds and long roads of the great outback far beyond New York, but they did much to put him securely on the national entertainment map. This was an ambiguous situation for Guthrie, and to the end of his career he remained uncomfortable with it: he thought of himself as more than an entertainer and conceived of his mission as more selfless than a career. He *was* an entertainer, though, and he *did* fitfully pursue an entertainer's career, but he remained one of the entertainment industry's most unpredictable and ornery captives, and his periodic "escapes" became part of the Guthrie legend.

Perhaps only slightly less important to his growing popularity was his work with the Almanac Singers, a storied group that served as the model for subsequent groups, from the Weavers to the New Christie Minstrels to Bob Dylan's Rolling Thunder Review. The Almanacs thought of themselves as traveling agents in the cause of social reconstruction, and basing themselves in New York's Greenwich Village, they toured the states, singing for union benefits and political rallies. As the war drew closer, their energies turned toward it, and they sang against fascism, both foreign and home-grown.

Guthrie continued this work on his own after the outbreak of war. He was now beamed to troops overseas by the Office of War Information, and his guitar had a sign on it that read, "This Machine Kills Fascists." After his enlistment in the Merchant Marine, the fascists, for their part, did their best to kill *him*; on two of his convoy trips across the Atlantic his ships were torpedoed.

Guthrie survived, and by the time the war was over he had become a national figure, not nearly of the stature of Bing Crosby, say, but still one with a steady following of those who either assented to his vision of a better America or who merely cottoned to his talent and his twangy voice. And now the bitterest of ironies: it was at this time of his life that the disease he had carried within him like a time bomb chose to express itself. In the late forties, he developed a strange, lopsided walk, and his speech occasionally slurred. He had been a hard drinker for much of his life, and the symptoms were attributed to alcoholism. Marjorie Guthrie, who now directs the Committee to Combat Huntington's Disease out of a small office in New York City, remembers with understandable regret that "We just didn't know enough about the disease in those days. It was only in retrospect many years later that I could see that what was happening to him had nothing to do with his drinking." For several years, as the disease continued the agonizingly slow deterioration of his nervous system, Guthrie signed himself in and out of hospitals as an alcoholic. His problem was not correctly diagnosed until, Marjorie recalls, 1954, and by then it was too late to do what little could have been done to delay the inevitable. In 1965 he was transferred from Brooklyn State Hospital to Creedmore State Hospital on Long Island. He never came out again.

In 1966—in the hospital—he was presented with the annual Conservation Service Award by Secretary of the Interior Stewart Udall. "Yours was not a passing comment on the beauties of nature," Udall wrote in the citation, "but a living, breathing, singing force in our struggle to use our land and save it, too."

On October 3, 1967, Woodrow Wilson Guthrie died.

Throughout that short and crowded life, in whatever medium or setting—between the covers of books, the lines of newspaper columns, over the radio, or in bars or union halls—Guthrie's intention was quite literally to sing for the silent ones. He had listened long and well to their talk, the accents, rhythms, and themes that fell casually from their lips and were lost. Their gift of spirit, he thought, was in their talk, and that talk put pictures in the poet's mind. Listening to a tubercular drifter's sandy, broken voice on some swirling Tucson street corner, "Lots of things went through your mind when he talked—wheat stems and empty cotton stalks, burnt corn, and eroded farm land."

These were the dark, faceless, shifting "strangers" seen at the edges of the cities, along the tracks and highways, in the fields. He sang them, their fractured narrative: gone with the seasons and the wind. Under a bridge out of the hard rain, an anonymous bindle stiff once shared his blanket with the minstrel but was gone in the morning before Guthrie ever saw his face or heard his name. "Tell me, / What were their names, tell me, what were their names," he sang in "The Sinking of the Reuben James."

I think here of an anecdote told by the Russian poet Anna Akhmatova out of the years of the Stalinist purges when she and other mothers and wives would wait day on day outside the gates of the prisons for word of those within. Once in that blue cold a woman recognized her and whispered a question in her ear: "Can you describe this?" And Akhmatova answered her, "Yes, I can."

This then was Woody's gift: to be able to describe the conditions, to give them shape, to sing for those millions who would never hear themselves, never get on the air or into print except as statistics.

And so to have this ability and to have the opportunity was a gift that imposed heavy obligations. Like his people, the minstrel was in perpetual debt. "The amount that we owe is all that we have," he observed once. And then went on to say that he had borrowed his words from his people, that the songs he sang were not his but theirs: "The only story that I have tried to write has been you." He wanted to mail himself like an urgent letter loaded with postage to those who otherwise would not read, to be like a wind-sent newspaper clipping that has a message and a picture of a man:

"And it was blow little paper, blow! Twist and turn and stay up as long as you can, and when you come down, come down on a pent-house porch, come down easy. . . . Come down and lay there in the rain and the wind and the soot and the smoke and the grit. . . . But keep on trying to tell your message, and keep on trying to be a picture of a man, because without that story and without that message printed on

you there, you wouldn't be much. Remember, it's just maybe, some day, sometime somebody will pick you up and look at your picture and read your message, and carry you in his pocket, and lay you on his shelf, and burn you in his stove. But he'll have your message in his head and he'll talk it and it'll get around."

He once signed himself with a drawing of a smoking pistol and the words "a desperate man, Woody Guthrie." A joke, maybe, but as always with him, beneath that there was the driven man with a mission that could never quite be fulfilled—because his country was itself unfulfilled. So he had to try to content himself with the conviction that his words were therapeutic, that they made a difference in the lives of those whose words he borrowed: "These songs say something about our hard traveling, something about our hard luck, our hard get-by, but the songs say we'll come through all these in pretty good shape, and we'll be all right. . . ."

And though the therapy of such songs was meant for the needy, plainly too it was meant for all America. These were not the faked songs of Hollywood and Tin Pan Alley with their prepackaged numbers about "champagne for two and moon over Miami." They were instead the real history of America, showing us the truth of ourselves, our squandering of precious human resources, the wasting of the American opportunity. Troubled, troublesome, a dealer in our common troubles, Woody Guthrie was still at last a classic American optimist, and it is just possible that the Guthrie revival we are now witnessing is a part of the long, slow process by which Americans assent to the best that is in us; a sign that we too are restless with the gap between our promises and our performance.

If this is in fact what nerves the Guthrie boom, it will be good: good for his memory, better for us. "The proof of the poet," Whitman wrote, "is that his country absorbs him as affectionately as he has absorbed it." And with Woody Guthrie that might also be the proof of the country.

Frederick Turner, whose "Terror of the Wilderness" appeared in our February, 1977, issue, teaches American Folklore and Literature at the University of Massachusetts and is editor of The North American Indian Reader.

Top: Woody during his brief stint in the Army, 1945. Bottom: taking the sun at Coney Island, about 1948.
COLLECTION OF MARJORIE GUTHRIE

*"I've sung this song, but I'll sing it again,
Of the people I've met and the places I've been.
Of some of the troubles that bothered my mind,
And a lot of good people that I've left behind, saying:
So long, it's been good to know ye,
So long, it's been good to know ye,
So long, it's been good to know ye,
What a long time since I've been home, and I've got to be drifting along."*

OF HUMAN RIGHTS...
AND WRONGS

DANIEL KRAMER

We Americans pride ourselves on our sophistication. We like to think that we are worldly-wise and cynical. We shed our milk teeth long ago, and if anyone appeals to our better impulses our instinctive response is to ask: Well, now, what's *his* angle?

It is a good pose, most of the time, and succeeding generations of sophomores have found it most effective. The trouble is that we can't keep it up. One of the enduring traits in the American character is the broad idealistic strain that was built in far back in the past, and it keeps coming to the surface when we least expect it. When this happens we feel embarrassed and try to act as if it were not happening.

Thus in the final quarter of the twentieth century—a century arranged to create cynicism, if one ever was—we find our President Carter reminding the rest of the world (in our name) that we are deeply and irrevocably concerned with human rights and that we get profoundly disturbed when we look about us and see areas where those rights are being violated.

A frequent response seems to be that this is dangerous, because some of the countries where human rights are most firmly denied are large and powerful and seem to take our President's remarks personally. Another response is a feeling that the man just ought not to go on that way because it is so dated; it is corny; say what you like in a Fourth of July oration, but don't mix patriotic rhetoric with sober statecraft or we may get involved in another "make the world safe for democracy" program before we have finished paying for the first one.

Finally, we have just a trace of guilt arising from the fact that there are places here in our own country where human rights are often given rather poor protection.

Yet what the President is doing is defending America in a world that has grown hostile. Words alone cannot be our first line of defense, but they can remind all hands what the great human values now at stake really are. We could stop talking, if our intellectual establishment finds the talk embarrassing, and resort to one clear alternative: a program of single-minded anticommunism.

We have given that alternative a rather extensive trial, and the result was not especially good. It led us straight into Vietnam, and we almost tore ourselves apart getting out. If there is a way to avoid doing something like that again, then we really ought to explore it.

There was a time, of course, when no one needed to talk about the human values that are involved in America's survival. People everywhere understood about them. They wanted those values in their own lives, and they proved it in the most direct way imaginable: by coming to America to live. They came by thousands, by tens of thousands, finally by millions, in the greatest folk migration the world has ever seen. They did not come over to make America different, and in the end they did not make it greatly different, although they did enrich it; they came because what America was drew them irresistibly.

It is necessary, of course, to remember that some of them experienced disappointment and disillusionment after they got here. The "melting pot" was imperfect, and many of the newcomers were royally exploited. It is also necessary to remind ourselves that black people came because they were forced and not because they wanted to, and for generations they had no freedom and no future. But over the long pull the people came, found a way to live that was better than what they had left behind, and learned to identify popular rights with being American.

It may be proper to remind ourselves that the same thing is true today. So many people want to get into the United States that along much of the border the effort to enforce immigration controls is in a state of virtual collapse. Something here draws them, and they come. If we do not practice everything that we preach, we make, by and large, a pretty good try.

It is also proper—indeed, it is downright essential—to remember that all of this began with words put down on paper. Maybe one of our problems today is that we do not spend enough time meditating on the Declaration of Independence. The preamble to that document is studded with by Bruce Catton

words that still contain fire, for us and for others—liberty, equality, the pursuit of happiness, unalienable human rights.

When they composed the Declaration, the Founding Fathers proclaimed that the sky was the limit. They interpreted the American dream in unforgettable terms, declaring that it meant a better life and a stake in society for *everyone*, regardless of race or sex or creed or previous conditions. The things the Declaration claimed for America were, by definition, things that all people everywhere were entitled to.

To put these words on paper and send them all across the world was to speak of more than America was prepared to deliver; but what the words called for could never be forgotten or ignored. They are still at work, those words, and if in troubled times like those of today an American President finds it advisable to remind us and everyone else just what we stand for, what we have been chiefly aiming at ever since we became an independent nation, who is to say that he is wrong? As a nation we may be grasping, materialistic, self-centered, forgetful, anything you like—but we built our country on a magnificent creed that bespeaks faith in humanity's ultimate destiny.

What we often overlook is that this faith expressed itself in a revolutionary new notion about where governments come from and what they rest on. In 1776 a national state and government drew its authority, its right to survive and rule, from delegations made willingly or otherwise by the kingship; from an entrenched ruling class, privileged in its ownership of land, wealth, and arms; from a general agreement that what the people got must come down from above and that the plain people were really pretty lucky to be allowed to exist at all.

The Declaration and later the Constitution turned this upside down, once and forever, by announcing flatly that the people *are* the state and the government, which have no other basis for existence.

Sovereignty belongs *only* to the people.

It belongs equally to all of them.

It allows neither for privileged orders nor for second-class citizens. It is not "handed down" by anybody; it exists because people exist.

Freedom, as a result, is defined quite simply as humanity's birthright. It goes with being a human being. It is totally and eternally unalienable. When anyone talks about human rights, that is chiefly what is meant. And although our country has its full share of imperfections—of failures to see the ideal, failures to grasp it, once seen, failures to live up to the high levels of achievement that we do reach now and then—freedom in the last analysis is what the existence of our country means.

That is why our remarks about the denial of human rights elsewhere in the world are listened to so attentively. Some governments are made nervous thereby, and it is easy to see why they are. What exists *here* is an ever-present reminder that what exists *there* does not need to be put up with, and when our President makes remarks about the denial of human rights—mild enough he has been about it, as a matter of fact—he is quietly reminding people of something.

It may well be that this course has certain dangers. Every course that anyone can suggest in this final quarter of the twentieth century has certain dangers, and it is not easy to see how this one is any more dangerous than all of the others. The hard fact is that we are in a time when it is necessary to live dangerously, and we might as well make up our minds to it. After all, in one way or another we have been doing it ever since the fourth day of July in 1776.

Freedom, we believe, is as much to be taken for granted as the air we breathe. Unfortunately, the air we breathe gets polluted over and again by the by-products of a highly mechanized society and the carelessness with which some of those by-products are used and disposed of. When that happens we complain about it, without first debating whether the complaint is politic, becoming to a great people, or likely to irritate strong folk who can be most unpleasant when roused. Why is what we are doing now any different? To say that freedom here and there is being polluted by despotism is right on a level with saying that the air is being polluted by industry and by our own heedlessness. Why should we expect a President of the United States to keep quiet about it?

It may be that one of our troubles is that we have spent the last twenty or thirty years giving ourselves a profound inferiority complex. We have scrutinized ourselves and our doings—properly enough, because we have made a number of king-sized errors—until we distrust our own motives. Most of all, we distrust our idealism and the people who still speak about it. We complain because human rights are denied elsewhere? Aha, what about our own record! Let us, cry the critics, put our own house in order before trying to remedy the world's ills.

That complaint might be valid, except that we call attention to the denial of human rights simply by existing. That, in the long run, is what America is all about. We can and will set our own house in order; review the record of the last half century if you don't believe it, and reflect that if much remains to do, a prodigious lot has actually been done. Meanwhile, even if our elected persons meekly keep as quiet as so many graven images, we still rebuke the deniers of human liberty.

What we are and what we mean speak with a voice that cannot be quieted.

SPALDING'S AUSTRALIAN BASE BALL TOUR.

Albert Spalding's middle name was Goodwill, which
seemed fitting in 1888 when the baseball
impresario and sporting goods king decided to take the
game on a grand tour to parts of the world as yet
unexposed to the glories of the American national
pastime. His own Chicago White Stockings and an All
America team drawn from both professional leagues
would play exhibition games around the globe. As the
group sailed from San Francisco, a journalist envisioned
"Baseball at Calcutta and Bombay, or on the Island of
Ceylon, where the branches of the sacred Bo tree might
form a natural grandstand. Perhaps the serene Lord
of all the Earth, the Emperor of Siam, may invite the
party to his court; and should he be pleased with the
game, he will no doubt present Mr. Spalding with a
genuine sacred white elephant." Such hyperbole was
not far off the mark; by the time "Spalding's Baseball
Tourists" sailed for home six months later, they had
dined with the king of Hawaii, exchanged toasts with
the ermine-robed mayor of Sydney, and chatted with
the future Edward VII, who later told the press that
while he thought baseball "an excellent game," he
considered cricket as "superior." In Rome the prelate
of the American College declared that with religion for
a bat and morality for an umpire his seminarians would
knock the ball evil over the fence, scoring a home run
each time.

The contests were cheered on five continents by
citizens of thirteen nations. Near the end of the tour
one reporter cabled home, "Only one continent now
remains to be subjugated by the American baseball bat.
Australia surrendered after a three weeks' campaign
of great brilliancy; Asia was met and overcome at
Colombo; Africa sent her forces up the Nile, only to be
overcome and brought to terms in the shadow of the
great pyramid. To-morrow we land in Europe, to begin
a triumphal march from Brindisi to Belfast. When the
Spalding party steams up New York harbor in the first
week of April they will come prepared to serve up the
whole earth on the home plate." As the two teams batted
the ball around the world it seemed as if the sun would
never set on a baseball game, but the impact of
Spalding's Tour was ephemeral. Today only Cuba and
Japan share our enthusiasm for the game, and neither
was on the 1888 itinerary. Still, Spalding pronounced
himself satisfied when he toted up the score and found
that expenses for the trip had just about been met by
the $50,000 in receipts.—C. D.

Spalding Bureau Base Ball Party, Chicago v.s. All America
at the Sphinx Feb 9 1889

At Cairo the players rode out on camels and donkeys to their ball park—the desert. The game's few spectators were curious fellahin who pounced on the ball whenever it came their way and proved unwilling to surrender it without a fight.

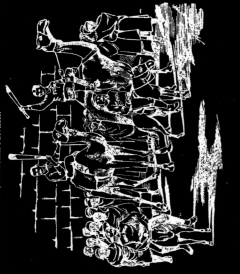

Temples of Democracy

The County Courthouse

by Calvin Trillin

This noble specimen of eclectic architecture, built in 1877-78, is the Davis County courthouse in Bloomfield, Iowa.
BOB THALL

There are 3,101 county courthouses in the United States, and a lot of history has happened in them. Abraham Lincoln was just one of hundreds of small-town lawyers who first made their marks in county courthouses, and scores of celebrated trials—from Lizzie Borden to Patty Hearst—have taken place inside them. Most of us have humbler courthouse errands—to file a deed, argue about a tax assessment, or buy a dog license.

Some of the buildings seem wonderfully incongruous now—ornate Renaissance-style palaces lording it over tiny cow towns; others are sadly anachronistic—turreted medieval fortresses in the bigger county seats, now dwarfed by glass and steel neighbors. Nor are they as central to our lives as they once were, since much of their power has leached away to state capitals and to Washington.

But they are still staunch hometown symbols of our faith in our ability to govern ourselves—and sometimes, too, of one county's determination to outshine the next.

As a Bicentennial project, the Seagram Company recently undertook to photograph county courthouses throughout America. Twenty-four photographers have produced over eight thousand photographs, covering more than a third of the existing buildings. Groups of the pictures will be exhibited around the country, and there will also be a book, Court House, *in which the cheerful essay by Calvin Trillin that appears on the following pages will serve as an introduction. Mr. Trillin is a staff writer for* The New Yorker. *The book will be edited by Richard Pare and published early next year by Horizon Press.*

Not since the Farm Security Administration recorded rural life in the 1930's has such a vast photographic documentation of America been attempted. As one of the photographers on the project said, "The buildings are a kind of temple of the community filled with icons of what people think government should be." Our portfolio, selected from the Seagram collection, suggests this American iconography.

The county courthouse—the one whose picture I carry in my mind—stands in the middle of a town square, with law offices pressing in on it like cocktail party guests bellying up to the hors d'oeuvres table. The building tries for height. The wide concrete stairs on the outside are high, and the ceilings are high, and, above the third floor, a high cupola displays on all four sides a clock that comes within fifteen or twenty minutes of telling everyone downtown the right time. Just inside the front door, a bulletin board displays the schedule of the circuit court and a notice about where to obtain crop-spraying advice and a poster from the Army recruiting service and a letter from the Department of Health, Education, and Welfare about food stamp eligibility and a brittle old piece of paper telling citizens what to do if they happen to be in the building paying their taxes or disputing their assessment at the moment of nuclear attack.

There are offices on either side of a broad hallway—with small signs, like old-fashioned lawyers' shingles, extending into the hall above each door to identify the county clerk or the county·treasurer or the county assessor. A wooden sign on the wall indicates with an arrow the direction of the jury room. The broad wooden steps leading to the second floor are bowed in the center from use. (A narrower flight of stairs leads down to the sheriff and his radio dispatcher and his jail in the basement, where there is no attempt at height.) On the second floor, court is in session. A lawyer with carefully tended sideburns and white patent-leather shoes is trying to explain why the skinny, miserable-looking teenage boy next to him should not be forever branded a felon merely because he yielded, just this one time, to the temptation of an unlocked Pontiac. The judge looks bored. The courtroom is otherwise empty except for the court clerk and the teen-ager's mother and a few elderly men who like to pass the time watching trials. On a bench outside the courtroom, a couple of men with tattoos and untended sideburns sit smoking, waiting their turn. Two or three small groups of people stand in the hall, each group dominated by a lawyer who is holding a fat brown file-envelope.

Downstairs, I enter the office of the county clerk. Printing on the frosted glass of the door identifies him once again by both name and title. I am there as a reporter from outside the county—to ask what the county clerk thinks about a dispute in the local schools or about the prospects of a murder defendant or about the fortunes of the local Democratic party (of which he happens to be the chairman). The county clerk's office has been modernized. The ceiling has been lowered and is made of white perforated squares. The walls have been covered in the sort of masonite made to simulate wood paneling. A couple of glass partitions mark off an office for the county clerk's secretary. There is no one at the secretary's desk. In a moment, the secretary returns. She has been at the vending machines that are tucked under the stairs. It is almost ten o'clock in the morning—time for her first Coke of the day.

When I worked as a newsmagazine reporter in the South, at the beginning of the sixties, everyone always seemed to be asking me where I was from. At the time, white people in the South preferred to believe that only ignorant and hopelessly vindictive Yankee reporters could portray racial turmoil as the product of genuine grievances rather than outside agitation. Loyalty to geography was assumed. County sheriffs seemed to have a particularly strong interest in my origins. "Where you from?" was always among the first questions a county sheriff asked. Often, he spoke while studying my press identification or my business card or even my driver's license (outside reporters occasionally had difficulty keeping their cars stationary at a stop sign long enough to qualify for what the local sheriff considered a full stop), and he sometimes ended the question with my first name, just to remind me where we stood. "I work out of the Atlanta bureau" was not considered an adequate response. That would only bring a sad shaking of the head and a loud "huh-uh." (There is no way to reproduce on paper the sound of a Southern sheriff's "huh-uh," but I suspect some philologist somewhere has classified it as the "adenoidal negative.") Then the sheriff would ask his second question: "Where you really from?" That meant "Where were you born?"

As it happens, I was born in Kansas City, Missouri. I could have done worse. The worst place to have been born was undoubtedly New York, the Center of Evil. If an outside reporter who had been born in New York was asked by a Southern sheriff where he was really from, the only sensible course open to him was perjury. In my case—my fellow stop-sign runners and I decided—there were better and worse ways to state the literal truth. Missouri, for instance, sounded less incriminating than Kansas City, only partly because Missouri had been a border state. To a

Southern sheriff, practically any state would have sounded less ominous than practically any city. A county would have sounded best of all.

For a lot of Americans, "county" still means country. It implies, at least, the absence of a big city. The county sheriff and the county courthouse are often identified with the South partly because the South remains the least urbanized region of the United States. There are, of course, places where "out in the county" refers to a collection of suburbs that elects a slick county executive to sit in a modernistic county center and fiddle slickly with zoning laws designed to keep out people no poorer than the Southern sheriffs who were interested in my birthplace. There are huge cities that conduct the business of the county seat in a downtown office building indistinguishable from the city hall; as it happens, Kansas City is one of them. But I think the picture of a county courthouse that a lot of Americans have in their minds is similar to my picture of the county courthouse in the town square. "County" still means country, and my best answer to the sheriff's question—if I had ever worked up the nerve to use it—would undoubtedly have been "Up around Jackson County, Missouri."

I once visited a copper town in Arizona that was about to lose its copper mine. The town was nestled in some mountains not far from the Mexican border, and the company in charge had, as mining people say, "recovered" just about all the copper that could be taken from the mountains at a profit. Architecturally, the town looked pretty much as it must have looked in the first decade or so of the century—partly because of some preservationist sentiment that is uncharacteristic of Western towns, and mostly because of some commercial lethargy that is quite characteristic of company towns. There were residents who believed that, once mining was over, the town—because of its quaint appearance and its splendid setting in the mined-out mountains—would prosper as an artists' colony or a tourist center. There were also residents who held out hope for the town simply because it was a county seat. In rural counties, the courthouse is an important industry. It provides not just county jobs but also lawsuits for lawyers and stationery orders for the office-supply store and repair work for the garage. It might mean a county hospital, and it is likely to mean a county newspaper. In the last century, tiny settlements often fought over designation as the county seat on the theory that the courthouse could mean survival. In this century, in areas

Clockwise from upper left: King William County, King William, Virginia, ca. 1725—the oldest continuously used courthouse in America; Tuscarawas County, New Philadelphia, Ohio, 1882-85; Buchanan County, St. Joseph, Missouri, 1873; Berks County, Reading, Pennsylvania, 1931-32; Caswell County, Yanceyville, North Carolina, 1858-61; Scott County, Winchester, Illinois, 1885

Two interiors: at left, the old St. Louis County courthouse, St. Louis, Missouri; below, Middlesex County courthouse, Cambridge, Massachusetts
LEFT: RICHARD PARE. BELOW: NICHOLAS NIXON

Jurors' chairs in Grady County
courthouse, Cairo, Georgia
JIM DOW

where rural counties have lost population to the cities, the theory still holds.

The district attorney is a county official even in cities so large that a gaggle of assistant district attorneys is required to keep up with the trial work. In those cities, an assistant district attorney often turns out to be a neatly dressed young man with winged-tip shoes who conducts the trial methodically, following a loose-leaf notebook he keeps on the table in front of him. Occasionally, a flashy assistant district attorney comes along to play to the courtroom buffs and cultivate the press—he is likely to specialize in pornography trials or the showier murders—but normally assistant district attorneys are relatively cautious about what they say outside as well as inside the courtroom. In criminal trials, reporters tend to be more comfortable with defense attorneys, who are often indiscreet enough to hint that their client is, in fact, guilty—the assumption being that a defense attorney who wins acquittal for a guilty client must be particularly brilliant. At lunch with a reporter after the jury goes out, a defense attorney may raise his martini and say, "To Justice—whoops, what am I saying! To Not Guilty." A defense lawyer can afford the style of a man not haunted by the prospect of having a victory reversed on appeal; there being no appeal from Not Guilty, he only has to win once. The caution of an assistant district attorney comes not only from the danger of reversible error but also from the conditions of his employment: a defense lawyer is engaged in private enterprise and an assistant district attorney is a man who works for the government.

In large counties, the district attorney tends not to do much trial work himself, husbanding his courtroom skills for the occasional case that happens to be politically significant or particularly juicy. In the late sixties, about the only case anybody in Houston could remember the district attorney of Harris County having tried personally was one in which Lee Otis Johnson, the noisiest black militant in town, was sentenced to thirty years in the penitentiary for allegedly giving away one marijuana cigarette. The most trial-wise district attorney that I ever met—a commonwealth's attorney officially, since that is what the D. A. is called in Kentucky—was a man named Daniel Boone Smith, who practiced his art for thirty or forty years in Harlan County, one of the Appalachian counties in the eastern part of the state. Smith, who seemed to be called Dan'l Boone by just about everyone in the county, was said to have tried more

capital cases than anyone in the history of the republic. Eight or nine years before I met him, Smith got curious about how many murder defendants he had prosecuted or defended—he did some defense work on the side in other counties—and his secretary counted up 750. Smith was able to amass a record like that partly because of longevity and partly because he was a quick worker ("Some people will take three days to try a murder case," he told me. "I usually try to get my case on in a day.") and partly because Harlan County, which used to be called Bloody Harlan, has traditionally offered a lot of opportunity for anyone interested in murder trials. Harlan County got to be known as Bloody Harlan in the thirties, when unions were trying to organize the mines, but mountain feuds had made it bloody long before that. Thirty years after the labor wars, Harlan had murders that often seemed the product of sudden drunken anger—one member of a family mowing down another who is breaking down the door trying to get at a third.

Smith, a man who knew his county, was renowned in eastern Kentucky for his ability to select a jury. In the urbanized counties of the Northeast, jury selection sometimes seems to be an exercise in ethnic studies. Is the Irish housewife a strong enough Catholic to take seriously what the Archbishop says about pornographic bookstores? Would the Polish construction worker be particularly anti-black or just normally anti-black? Does that Italian or Jewish grandfather have the sort of warm family feeling that would make him particularly sympathetic to the survivors of a young person killed needlessly in an auto crash? In a place like Harlan County, Kentucky, jury selection has a lot to do with local history—remembering which prospective juror's uncle may have had a boundary dispute with which witness's grandfather twenty years before. Daniel Boone Smith knew his local history. He also knew how to talk to eastern Kentucky jurors—how to get his point across with a personal recollection or a country anecdote that had Dan'l Boone Smith as the butt. Hearing him talk to a jury—hearing him recall old Uncle Bob Woolford who used to work up at Evarts or describe a case he once had over at Coldiron—it was hard to keep in mind that he was, as he confessed to me shortly after we met, a graduate of Harvard Law School.

Until the early sixties, all Democratic primaries in Georgia were operated under something called the County Unit System. The Democratic primary was the only primary that counted, of course, since

the Republican nomination for state office at the time was, as the county politicians would have said, "not worth a bucket of warm spit." Under the County Unit System, carrying a county, by whatever margin, gave the candidate unit votes that varied according to the population of the county—the kicker being that the largest county in the state had only six votes and the smallest county had two. There are 159 counties in Georgia, and some of them, it is sometimes said, amount to no more than a courthouse and a speed trap. Even the smallest one had a third the vote of Atlanta. When Gene Talmadge was running for governor, he used to say that he never bothered to campaign in a county large enough to have a streetcar.

The years just before the federal court finally struck down the County Unit System were particularly frustrating for the civic leaders of Atlanta, who were then trying to build the city's reputation as a progressive commercial center that was, in the words of its mayor, William B. Hartsfield, "too busy to hate"—a slogan I always thought of as Babbittry Over Bigotry. Atlanta boosters were embarrassed at being represented in Congress by a distinctly nonprogressive type named James Davis, who, because of the County Unit System, could win the nomination every two years even without carrying the city. Judge Davis, as he was always called, was not too busy to hate. In fact, he struck people in Washington as the sort of man who would drop anything he happened to be doing if a good opportunity for hating came along.

In 1960, Mayor Hartsfield finally got so irritated at Davis' continual nomination that he ran an ape against him in the general election. The ape lived in the Atlanta zoo and was himself named Willie B., after the mayor. Hartsfield held a press conference at the zoo to introduce Willie B. and compare his progress on the scale of political evolution favorably with that of Judge Davis. Willie B. actually received a few hundred votes. On election night, a sign in the city room of the Atlanta Constitution said, "Vote for Willie B.—Let Us Begin Again."

I once attended an auction of land sold for taxes at the Costilla County courthouse, in San Luis, Colorado. Costilla County was settled by Spanish-Americans from around Taos and Chama, in northern New Mexico, who came in the 1850's as pobladores, or settlers, on something called the Sangre de Cristo land grant. The courthouse, a plain, one-story building of adobe, was built in 1870. Some of its offices have

The judge—Licking County courthouse,
Newark, Ohio
LEWIS S. KOSTINER

FRANK GOHLKE

LEWIS S. KOSTINER

LEWIS S. KOSTINER

WILLIAM CLIFT

GEOFF WINNINGHAM

WILLIAM CLIFT

Interior details, clockwise from upper left: Hennepin County, Minneapolis, Minnesota; Hamilton County, Noblesville, Indiana; Bent County, Las Animas, Colorado; Hinsdale County, Lake City, Colorado; Hill County, Hillsboro, Texas; Chaffee County, Salida, Colorado

been modernized, but the courtroom, where the land auction was being held, looked pretty much the way it must have looked in the nineteenth century. It did have electricity—a couple of naked lightbulbs hanging from the ceiling by electric cords. The walls of the courtroom were bare except for what seemed to be a large square of upholstery fabric taped behind the judge's chair—provided, I gathered, so that the judge could, during slow summations, tilt back and lean his head comfortably against the wall.

The county clerk, who was acting as auctioneer, would describe each parcel in some detail, often continuing the description from his own knowledge after he finished reading what was on the official list. Some of the parcels went for as little as fifteen or twenty dollars. I happened to be in Costilla County because of an argument over the use of a 67-thousand-acre tract of land that had been purchased for $500,000—an argument about whether the descendants of the *pobladores* had hunting and grazing and gathering rights even though an outsider had bought and obtained clear title to the land. The county clerk could also describe that tract without reference to notes. So could the county treasurer. It was all there in the courthouse—the deed and the surveys and the correspondence over assessment disputes and the tax receipts.

Land—real estate—is often at the center of disputes around the country, although normally not as overtly as in the Costilla County controversy. Usually, the argument seems on the surface to be about industrial development or the environment or schools or highway construction, but in the background is often the question of who owns what real estate and how its value will be affected by what happens. The county courthouse keeps score.

County Sheriff is a job that comes with not only a salary and a police cruiser but a persona. The folklore that clings to a county sheriff is strong—the fearless sheriff seen in Western films, the fearsome sheriff seen in Southern civil rights demonstrations. In New England, where the sheriff is often just the man in charge of the jail, I have seen sheriffs who could be mistaken for the county clerk or an assistant district attorney, but most of the sheriffs I have met look like sheriffs. They wear a star. They wear a wide-brimmed hat. They often wear boots. They like large silver belt buckles. A lot of sheriffs walk alike and talk alike and wear their stomachs over their gun belts in the same style. A sheriff I once knew in Cole County, Missouri, outraged an Iranian

exchange student who wouldn't walk to his cell on his own two feet by saying, in what I have come to think of as a Sheriff Accent, "Well, jus' lay there you damn Commanus." The student's anger at being called a Communist, I decided, was based on the assumption that the word was meant to describe political ideology; he didn't realize that a county sheriff might call a man a Communist as an alternative to calling him a sissy or a yellow dog. A lot of sheriffs—compassionate sheriffs as well as brutal sheriffs, sophisticated sheriffs as well as xenophobic sheriffs—do a Sheriff Act.

I suppose there are sheriffs these days who wear double-knit suits and sheriffs with computerized headquarters and even sheriffs who act like those coldly polite, sharply creased state troopers who call everybody "sir" while continuing to complete the required report. But the sheriff whose picture I carry in my mind looks something like the sheriff of Cole County, Missouri—a man I once described as having "an old-fashioned county-sheriff speech pattern that tends to relax the formality of his headquarters, as well as an old-fashioned county-sheriff build that tends to tighten the pressure on the lower buttons of his shirt." He is asking me where I am really from. And I am telling him that I am really from right there in Missouri—over around Jackson County. ☆

"Don't ever tell me that a woman cannot be called to preach the Gospel," she once wrote. "If any man ever went through one hundredth the part of hell on earth that I lived in, they would never say that again." If hell was the hopelessness of poverty, Aimee Semple McPherson had been there. But she preached her way out of those depths, and by the time of her death had ascended into a heaven of wealth and power.

She was born Aimee Elizabeth Kennedy in 1890 on a little farm near the town of Ingersoll, Ontario, Canada. Her mother, a tambourine-thumping Salvation Army veteran, dedicated Aimee, then six weeks old, to the work of God. She remained true to that dedication until adolescence, when the doctrines of Darwin and the temptations of the secular world temporarily mired her in the quicksand of unbelief. But under the weighty ministrations of a Pentacostal preacher, Robert Semple, Aimee found herself born again. She burned her ragtime sheet music, her novels, and dancing pumps, and married Semple. A few months later, the newlyweds were off to China as missionaries.

Within a year, Robert Semple was dead of dysentery, and eighteen-year-old Aimee found herself back in New York, penniless and with a baby. In desperation she married Harold McPherson, and by him she had another child. But her

WIDE WORLD

by William B. Hamilton

intractable will, buttressed by a commanding religious experience, could not long stand marital bliss, and she took to the road as a traveling evangelist.

Aimee ran her own show. She drove her own tent pegs, played her own piano, and developed her own evangelistic techniques as she traveled up and down the Atlantic coast with her children and her mother. Several years on this glory road persuaded Aimee it was time for a change, and in 1918, with $100 and a broken-down car, her little band rolled into Los Angeles.

Except for a few local revivals in upstairs mission rooms, Los Angeles was, at first, just a base from which Aimee toured the area with limited success. But her luck changed when she went to San Diego, then home of the ill and incurable, city of suicides. Thirty thousand people attended an open-air meeting sponsored by local churches. While Aimee held forth, a paralytic woman rose from her wheelchair and stumbled toward the platform. Near hysteria followed as scores of sick and crippled San Diegans surged forward. Aimee had never claimed she could heal the sick, but her fame as a healer quickly spread up and down the Pacific Coast, and riding this crest, she returned to Los Angeles determined to build a church.

Los Angeles in the 1920's was, according to many contemporary observers, a cuckoo land with more sanctified cranks to the acre than any other town in America. It was also a city of strangers; more than a million and a quarter newcomers entered the county during the decade. Aimee fit right in. Before long, she had acquired more than fifty thousand followers—enough to enable her to build Angelus Temple, a hugh cakelike structure that cost over a million and a half dollars. It was equipped with a powerful radio station and topped with an illuminated rotating cross that could be seen for fifty miles. In the following years, Sister Aimee established over four hundred branch churches, or "lighthouses," and sponsored 178 mission stations throughout the world.

The cause of Aimee's success was not her so-called Foursquare Gospel: biblical infallibility, conversion, religious healing, and the imminent return of Christ. It was her vibrant personality, unconventional preaching, and, especially, her flair for drama and publicity that won her the loyalty—and money—of her people. Aimee gave them a show, and they were willing to pay for it. Angelus Temple was fitted out with a stage on which Sister enacted sacred operas and religious tableaux. Dancing devils complete with hellfire and pitchforks were routed before the eyes of the assembly by the godly gunfire of Aimee's Army. Flowers, music, pageantry, and sex appeal were the props behind Aimee's message of joy, but she was always the star.

Then, on a sparkling May morning in 1926, she went for a swim at a Los Angeles beach—and disappeared. "Aimee McPherson believed drowned!" screamed the newspaper headlines. Her stunned mother was sure her soul was with Jesus. But where was her body? Divers combed the shoreline, motor launches with grappling hooks swept the deeper water, and airplanes circled overhead. For thirty-two days armies of the faithful kept constant vigil at beach and Temple. A memorial service was held, and the sorrowing throng parted with over $34,000 in their grief. Three days later came a call from Douglas, Arizona. Aimee was alive. She allegedly had been kidnapped.

Aimee's explanation was a lusty combination of intrigue, torture, and sex, climaxed by a hair-raising escape and a triumphant return to safety. The public loved it, but the police failed to find the kidnappers' hut in which she claimed to have been held, let alone the kidnappers. Other discrepancies in Sister's story resulted in Aimee's indictment and trial on charges of conspiracy to obstruct justice. The theory was that she had engineered her own vanishing act in order to run off with Kenneth Ormiston, a long-time Temple radio operator—and a married man. After four months, however, the charges against Aimee were dropped—leaving no one satisfied. To this day, the full story of Aimee's "kidnapping" remains unknown.

Failing in her attempt to find a life away from her Temple, she directed her formidable energies back into the Temple itself—with sometimes explosive results. Family infighting over Temple monetary policies resulted in a broken nose for Sister's mother and a lawsuit against Aimee by her own daughter—and fifty-five additional lawsuits by disgruntled followers and employees hounded her for the rest of her career. But Aimee was still Aimee, never one to let the Devil get her down. Paris fashions, face lifts, and new religious theatrics kept the Temple jumping and Aimee before the public eye. Her death from an overdose of barbiturates in 1944 came as a severe shock to the thousands of people who had found in Aimee's life some of the color and joy lacking in their own. Fifty thousand mourners viewed her as she lay in state on the platform of Angelus Temple, reclining in a bronze casket with her hands clasped over an open Bible, and a caravan of six hundred cars followed "the mistress of hallelujah revivalism," as the *London Daily Mail* called her, to her final resting place in Forest Lawn Memorial Park. "Today," her eulogist intoned, "we are here to commemorate the stepping up of a country girl to God's Hall of Fame."

MARKS FOR THE MARKETPLACE

The Curious World of the Trademark

by Gerald Carson

Millions of readers have been pleasured by the writings of John Steinbeck, but there was no joy in the Atlanta headquarters of the Coca-Cola Company when the Pulitzer-prize-winning novelist's *The Wayward Bus* reached the executive suite.

" 'You rather have a coke?' " asked the traveling salesman who was trying to move in on the blonde at the bus stop lunchroom.

" 'No. Coffee,' " she replied. " 'Cokes make me fat.' "

" 'Got any coke?' " another character asked.

" 'No,' " said the proprietor. " 'Few bottles of Pepsi-Cola. Haven't had any coke for a month. It's the same stuff. You can't tell them apart.' "

It was bad enough from the Coca-Cola point of view to violate the company's famous trademark (which covers both Coca-Cola and Coke) by using the lower-case "c" instead of capitalizing the name. The error was compounded when Steinbeck also used the plural form. Such usages denigrate a trademark by implying that it is not unique but represents a class of goods. Then, to cap it all, there was that untoward comparison with Pepsi-Cola.

Nor could the General Foods Corporation have been any less distressed than the Coca-Cola management if its officers read the description in *The Wayward Bus* of what was on the third shelf behind the counter of the luncheonette. For there were stacked "individual boxes of . . . grapenuts, and other tortured cereals." They caught the eye of Mr. Pritchard, a businessman and one of the passengers on the bus. After ordering breakfast for his wife and daughter, he said, " 'I'll have grapenuts and cream. . . .' "

Grape-nuts is, of course, a historic, valuable, and diligently guarded trademark of General Foods. The risk it was exposed to by the wayward novelist is highlighted by a remark that Mrs. Pritchard made when she felt a headache coming on. " 'Elliott,' " she said to her husband, " 'see if they have any aspirins, will you?' " They did, and the woman behind the counter obligingly tore a "cellophane bag" off a display card and handed it to the indisposed lady.

What is at issue here, then, is that Coca-Cola, Coke, and Grape-nuts must be capitalized and handled carefully with respect to property rights, while it is perfectly correct to lower-case aspirin and cellophane—to which may be added zipper, thermos, linoleum, mimeograph, yo-yo, and literally scores of other once-proud names that have slipped into the English language and have

Victrola

"Coke" is the abbreviation for Coca-Cola —the registered trade-mark which identifies only the product of— THE COCA-COLA COMPANY

The price of supersalesmanship: The exclusivity of a trademarked name can easily become endangered, the result— paradoxically—of heavy advertising. Consumers often apply the name of one specific product to another of the same type, so companies such as Coca-Cola and the others whose trademarks and trademarked products appear on these pages maintain batteries of vigilant lawyers, always on the lookout for trademark transgressions.

LEFT: ARCHIVES, THE COCA-COLA COMPANY, ATLANTA, GA.
BELOW: CULVER

become merely the common description of a whole category of products but no longer of any particular one.

The story of this fall from grace begins with the legal character of a trademark and a glance at social and economic history. A trademark is, quite simply, a mark of somebody's trade. It is defined today in U.S. statutory law as including "any word, name, symbol, or device, or any combination thereof adopted and used by a manufacturer or merchant to identify his goods and distinguish them from those manufactured or sold by others." The mark is an indication of origin, of quality, or at least of uniformity, and often carries the suggestion of inherent characteristics that may give the product an edge in the marketplace. For example, Halo, the name of a shampoo, conveys the pleasant idea of soft highlights in the hair; Talon suggests that a particular slide fastener will do well what it is supposed to do in gripping and holding.

"Brand" or "brand name" are colloquial terms often used as synonyms for "trademark," but "trade name" means something quite different. A trade name is the name of the maker, not of the product. General Motors Corporation is a trade name, Cadillac a trademark. Jell-O is a trademark, but General Foods, owner of

the Jell-O mark, is a trade name. Most trade names would not pass the trademark examiner at the Patent Office as being registrable. But there are exceptions. Johnson & Johnson is both a trade name and a trademark, and the "Celanese" portion of Celanese Corporation is a trademark.

Trademark protection, since it provides the legal basis for fending off unfair competition, is a valuable right. Without it, our modern industrial society would be in chaos and the consumer at the mercy of a host of con men. The encroachment is called infringement and was well defined by Judge Augustus N. Hand in 1952. When a manufacturer of children's shoes and related items introduced the mark Gro Pals after R. H. Macy & Co., Inc., the big New York department store, had long used the marks Gro-Shoe and Gro-Sock, the U.S. Court of Appeals granted Macy's an injunction stopping the sale of Gro Pals. In delivering the court's opinion Judge Hand said, "Infringement is based on the existence of similarity such as would cause confusion of any appreciable number of ordinarily prudent purchasers as to the source of the goods," and he added that it was hard to avoid the conclusion that "there was a deliberate purpose to obtain some advantage from the trade which Macy had built up."

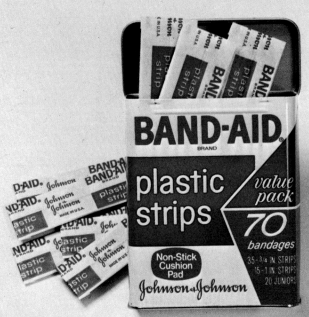

Infringement can be stopped even if there is no intention to confuse the purchaser and even if the products of the two firms are not competitive, provided, in the latter case, that the newcomer is clearly trying to borrow the advertising and good will of the trademark owner. It would be folly, for instance, for a manufacturer to come out with a Kodak bicycle.

It is small wonder, then, that the statistics of trademark registrations are impressive. The total issued in the United States alone stands at 1,067,920, with about half a million marks on the active register. In 1976, the last year for which figures are available, 40,117 applications were filed and 29,208 registrations issued.

Distinctive marks as indicia of ownership appear in the famous cave paintings of southwestern Europe, where cattle are shown with brand marks on their flanks, and pottery four thousand years old has been found around the Mediterranean littoral with the maker's emblem on the handle. In the Middle Ages merchant marks were placed upon pewter, cloth, gold and silver articles, even baker's bread, not as a right of the seller but as a liability imposed upon the merchant or guild to protect the buyer against fraud. Justice could be summary. In the Palatinate in the fourteenth century an innkeeper was hanged for passing off cheap wine as Rüdesheimer.

It was recognized that the marks were of prime economic importance to the maker or seller, and many fanciful house marks incorporating animals, hearts, seals, Christian symbols, initials, and cyphers came to be used by rich merchants as a kind of bourgeois heraldry, then evolved into coats of arms when the traders became gentlemen. Some of these symbols of trade may still be seen in the brasses and stained-glass windows of ancient colleges, abbeys, and cathedrals of England and Europe.

But it was not until producer and consumer were no longer in close contact, that is to say, not until about the middle of the nineteenth century—when mass production and distribution of consumer goods made a merchandising shortcut imperative—that the use and true value of trademarks were fully appreciated, although trademark protection in England was first enacted into law in 1783. In the United States a statute providing for the registration of marks was passed in 1870 and revised in 1876, but was struck down three years later by the Supreme Court as being unconstitutional. A new law was enacted in 1881, replaced by others in 1905, 1920, and 1946. Under them, trademarks assumed their modern function as a form of "commercial magnetism," in Justice Felix Frankfurter's phrase, to draw customers to the article or commodity upon which the "congenial symbol" appears.

Today famous brand names are part of the American vernacular. We know them, too, by their visual images. They are like old friends: Leo, the MGM lion, White Rock's Psyche, the bearded Smith Brothers of cough-drop fame, American Telephone and Telegraph's bell, Prudential's Rock of Gibraltar, and Planters' Mr. Peanut, that vivacious, swaggering, top-hatted figure—that jaunty boulevardier with monocle and cane who, because of the

whirligig of national politics, now enjoys the prestige of association with the White House. Goobers are so definitely "in" that an enterprising entrepreneur of Plains, Georgia, began peddling bottles of peanut soil for five dollars, and peanut soup became the soupe du jour every Wednesday at Washington's luxury hotel, the Sheraton-Carlton.

A trademark may be a coined word (Kleenex), a family name (Schlitz), the mark of a service (Greyhound); it may even be suggestive, provided it is not descriptive (Coppertone). The suggestive mark hints fancifully of a desirable characteristic of the product but does not describe it: a "Mallard" raincoat reminds one of how a duck sheds water. The idea for a trademark may come from almost anywhere—from a scientific survey, an employee contest, a "think tank," a brainstorming session, an encyclopedia, a sudden inspiration. A computer came up with the name for the world's largest oil company—Exxon. The double x is especially helpful since it is a combination found only in the Maltese language and a few English surnames.

"You need a name," said a paper-box manufacturer in a meeting with executives of a baking company many years ago when packaged, trademarked, nationally advertised food products were still a novelty in this country.

"You needa... Uneeda Biscuit!" Henry N. McKinney, an advertising man who had already christened Keds, Karo, and Meadow Gold Butter, is credited with saying. Thus suddenly a historic brand name came into existence.

Or take, as another example, the case of a small company in St. Paul whose principal product was sandpaper. In 1925 little Minnesota Mining and Manufacturing (3M) addressed itself to a big problem of the Detroit automobile giants. Two-tone body finishes were the hot news in car styling, made possible by the invention of quick-drying lacquers and automatic spray guns. But the automobile factories could not get a sharp edge where the colors met.

Something was needed that would stick and hold, seal off paint solvents, yet come off easily. It seemed that 3M had the answer—a two-inch-wide masking tape backed, along both edges, with a narrow strip of adhesive. The adhesive was only a quarter of an inch wide. This appealed to the 3M management because it lowered production costs to omit the stickum on the middle part of the tape. One edge of the tape was applied to the car body, the other gripped the masking paper. But—the tape failed to hold. A

POLLY PUT THE KETTLE ON
WE'LL ALL MAKE
JELL-O

wrathy foreman of a paint shop turned on a 3M salesman and said: "Take this tape back to your stingy Scotch bosses and tell them to put more adhesive on it."

The home office got the point, corrected the error, and someone with a sense of humor bestowed the name Scotch brand on the tape. Thus the Scotch concept, strengthened by a tartan design, became a valuable trademark suggesting satisfaction and economy, and has since been applied to hundreds of the products of this high-technology company.

Some marks, which incorporate words like "Royal," "Premier," "Black and White," or "Star," are rated as "weak" because they are common descriptive adjectives and so other companies may appropriate them in other fields without incurring any legal liability whatsoever. Castle & Cooke, one of the famous "five companies" of Hawaii, sold macadamia nuts under the brand name "Royal Hawaiian" and claimed infringement when another corporation applied for registration of the same term for a line of liqueurs. But the Patent Office rejected the argument. It ruled that there was no reasonable likelihood that purchasers would get confused between Royal Hawaiian liqueurs and Royal Hawaiian nuts, so the liquor company was entitled to register the

trademark for its own field of products.

Other marks are rated as "strong" because they are distinctive, original, fanciful, and set the product apart from all others. Aunt Jemima is one of these, but the classic example is Kodak. The name was thought up by George Eastman to identify his cameras and camera supplies. Philologically the word is meaningless—and startlingly abrupt. "Bitten off by consonants at both ends," one trademark historian has written, "it snaps like a 'Kodak' shutter."

Whether they are strong or weak, all trademarks must be watched over and policed because of a paradox. They can be *too* successful, in that their very success may lead ultimately to their demise. This occurs when a brand name becomes so completely connected in the public mind with a whole class of articles— whether it be cosmetics, cereals, vacuum cleaners, chewing gum, or whatever—that the purchaser regards it as being the name of the type of product, not of a specific one. At that point, which is usually determined by a court test, exclusiveness can slip away entirely and the legal rights in the brand name are destroyed forever. When the owner of a trademark lets down the guard to that extent, Dorothy Fey, executive director of the United States

Stain-proof – Spot-proof – Easily cleaned
LINOLEUMS

Trademark Association, calls the result "Genericide."

Some precautions for protecting a mark from becoming generic are:

The name should be capitalized. If it is written in lower case, the name should be enclosed by quotation marks.

Since a trademark is a proper adjective, it should, wherever possible, be followed by the common name (noun) of the product, as in Band-Aid brand *adhesive bandages* or Pyrex brand *glassware*. There are occasional exceptions, as when the consumer understands beyond the shadow of a doubt. A Buick is a Buick. Nor does Procter & Gamble need to say that Tide is a detergent in every printed advertisement.

If the trademark is registered, all printed matter should make that fact clear. There are several acceptable ways of doing this, the shortest and simplest being the association of the trademark with a capital R in a circle: ®. Danger signals are the use of the possessive, "nouning," "verbing," and the appearance of the plural. "Please don't use our name in vain. Use it the way the good law intended," the Xerox Corporation pleads; and when former Senator Sam J. Ervin, Jr., chairman of the Watergate investigating committee, spoke casually of "xeroxing" some material during the televised hearings, he received a courteous but educative letter from the Xerox people on trademark grammar.

Many firms have standard letters ready to be sent when necessary to writers, the distributors that handle their merchandise, the general public, and lexicographers, thanking them politely for their interest in the product but chiding them for sinning against the law of trademarks. Company executives are precise in speaking, careful in writing even the most informal internal office communications. They issue instruction pamphlets and schedule special advertising campaigns in publications read by editors and journalists. "*Only* Dow makes Styrofoam brand insulation and buoyancy billets!" the Dow Chemical Company pointed out in an advertisement. "Please, hit that capital S when typing Styrofoam or mark it UC [upper case] on proofs. . . . Thank you."

The ghostly presence of shredded wheat, lanolin, celluloid, dry ice, and milk of magnesia haunts marketing men and makes compulsive dictionary-watchers of corporate executives who may read and ponder when they find Frigidaire and Jell-O in the *American Heritage Dictionary* carefully capitalized and defined as trademarks, while cellophane, which took twelve years of time plus untold sums of money and great toil to win its place in the sun

after being introduced from France, languishes in lower-case ignominy as just a type of wrapping material made from wood pulp. Common property. A household word. Both the Frenchman who invented cellophane, and du Pont de Nemours and Company, which bought the U.S. rights to manufacture it, constantly and inexplicably used the coined name in a descriptive sense; the company, for one thing, used the name as referring to a class of cellulose products, not a unique brand emanating from du Pont. (It was the same mistake that the Otis Elevator Company made when in its advertising it used the trademark "Escalator" in conjunction with the common word "elevator.")

And so, when du Pont challenged a competitor in court for filling orders for cellophane, it lost. The word, freed of all ties, went into the English language. *Sic transit gloria mundi* in the world of business when the proprietary trade term of a careless owner gets *too* popular.

Gerald Carson has frequently written for AMERICAN HERITAGE *on business and economic subjects. His most recent book,* The Golden Egg: The Personal Income Tax; Where it Came From, How it Grew, *was published last spring by Houghton Mifflin Company.*

"I AM BECO

The Agony of J. Robert Oppenheimer

IE DEATH..."

by Richard Rhodes

In the life of J. Robert Oppenheimer—the American physicist and scientist-statesman who directed the building of the first atomic bombs at Los Alamos, New Mexico, during World War II, whose government, discerning "fundamental defects" in his character, denied him security clearance in 1954, who died of throat cancer in 1967—some have professed to see embodied the moral ambiguities of twentieth-century science, science charging breakneck over human institutions, scientists waking compromised from Faustian dreams. These are tabloid notions, but Oppenheimer did live at the center of the century's most disturbing contradictions, and struggled with them, and suffered for them, and if he is often taken as their protagonist, it is partly because he was a man of disturbing contradictions himself.

He was an authentic genius, the brightest of his generation, who never earned a Nobel Prize and to whose name no seminal scientific contributions today attach; a man of fierce, lively energy who brooded endlessly on death; a man of great personal warmth and devotion whose colleagues say they never knew him well; a man of gentleness who frequently lashed out with contemptuous sarcasm to cause others pain; a man of integrity who voluntarily sacrificed many of his students and friends to the Torquemadan mercies of Army Counter-Intelligence and the FBI; a loyal patriot who was subjected to public humiliation at McCarthyesque hearings and whose security clearance, once denied, was never, to the end of his life, restored; a man dedicated more profoundly than most men to peace who helped inflict on the world its most terrifying instruments of war. Some of these contradictions have been, or can be, resolved. Others may never be, because he reserved his privacy as rigorously as did Thomas Jefferson, whose reach of mind his own resembled. But like all men—like Jefferson, too—J. Robert Oppenheimer left behind his tantalizing clues.

He was born to prosperity working up to wealth, in New York City, on April 22, 1904. Three Van Goghs, a Picasso, a Renoir would decorate the living room of his family's spacious apartment by the time he left for Harvard. According to his birth certificate, he was christened Julius Robert; he carried through life only the initial, insisting it stood for nothing at all, but Julius was his father's name. Julius Oppenheimer, a vigorous and idealistic man, had emigrated from Germany in 1887 to join his uncle's textile-importing firm and at age thirty, in 1900, became a partner. He married Ella Friedman in 1903.

Robert Oppenheimer's mother was beautiful and a painter. She had studied impressionist technique in Paris and taught from her own studio in New York. She wore long sleeves always, and a chamois glove; her right hand was congenitally unformed. She was loving but severely disciplined, a descendant of a dignified Baltimore family; she engendered in her son, by the time he grew to be a man, a courtliness that even Europeans sometimes found extravagant; in her presence no one presumed to raise his voice. "I was an unctuous, repulsively good little boy," Oppenheimer said later. "My childhood did not prepare me for the fact that the world is full of cruel and bitter things. It gave me no normal, healthy way to be a bastard."

The Oppenheimers' second child, Lewis, born in Robert's infancy, died soon after birth, and horrified of germs and perhaps in retreat from that bereavement, they guarded Robert from companions and the street. He was a frail child, frequently ill, frequently lonely, precociously sensitive, precociously bright. When Robert was five, Julius took him to Germany to visit his Grandfather Ben; Ben praised Julius' success and gave his blue-eyed grandson a rock collection. It was Robert's first recorded glimpse of science: science at its most modest, classifying, and science at its most inanimate, rocks. He carried his collection home and enlarged it, his father indulgently supplying funds, until specimens lined the apartment halls. And that early in the involution of his aesthetics, or in his extreme isolation, he barricaded himself behind essences. He chose to specialize in crystals, atomic signatures cleaved to immutable geometries, certainties of rock that without genealogy, uncreatured, are born and perfect themselves and reproduce. He specialized so fervently that the curator of crystals at the New York Museum of Natural History took him as a pupil. A professional microscope that he tuned to the enormities of minutiae was his other childhood toy.

Once he learned to read, he lived in books, encountering there his peers. When he was old enough for classrooms he attended New York's Ethical Culture School, the fine pedagogic extension of Felix Adler's Society for

Ca. 1906

Ethical Culture to which Julius Oppenheimer belonged, which declared that "man must assume responsibility for the direction of his life and destiny": man, as opposed to God. Robert did: did laboratory experiments in the third grade, began keeping scientific notebooks in the fourth, began studying physics in the fifth, lectured to the surprised and then delighted members of the New York Mineralogical Club when he was twelve.

At fourteen, to get him out of doors and perhaps to help him find friends, his parents sent him to camp. He walked the trails of Camp Koenig looking for rocks and, with the only friend he found, discoursing on George Eliot, emboldened by her conviction that cause and effect ruled human affairs. The other boys labeled him "Cutie," and when casual bullying elicited no response hauled him off one night to the icehouse, stripped him bare, beat him up—"tortured him," his friend said—and painted his genitals and buttocks green. Responsibly he stuck it out until camp ended, never went back, never mentioned the place or the humiliation again. But, not yet fifteen, he told a teacher at Ethical that fall, "I'm the loneliest man in the world."

The loneliest man in the world graduated as Ethical's valedictorian in February, 1921. In late April, waiting for his younger brother, Frank, born in 1912, to finish school so that the Oppenheimer family could summer in Europe, he underwent surgery for appendicitis. Recovered from that, while rock hunting in the Harz Mountains he contracted severe colitis. It laid him up for months, too ill to enter Harvard with his class; determined to toughen him, his father sent him off shortly after Christmas with a sturdy Ethical English teacher for a tour of the West. At the Los Pinos dude ranch, in the Sangre de Cristo Mountains northeast of Santa Fe, he learned to ride horses and live in rain and weather.

Like Eastern semi-invalids in the frontier days, Oppenheimer's encounter with wilderness, freeing him from civilized restraints, was decisive, a healing of faith. In the years to come he would lease a ranch in the Sangre de Cristos up near ten thousand feet, and he and Frank would ride a thousand miles on horseback in a summer, sometimes ranging as far away as Colorado, living on raisin chocolate and whiskey and Vienna sausages and cheese. "My two great loves," he wrote a friend in 1929, "are physics and the desert. It's a pity they can't be combined." Eventually he contrived to combine them, siting the bomb laboratory, the ethical Erewhon, across the Rio Grande from the mountains, on Los Alamos, a desert mesa extended from below the rim of an ancient and exemplary caldera, a narrow, canyon-cut plateau eroded from the throe of the most violent extinct volcano in the world.

He came back tanned to Harvard, he said, like a Goth coming into Rome, and ravished it. He carried six courses at a time—the requirement was five—and audited four more. He read *The Waste Land*, just published, and saw himself reflected, and began to seek the stern consolation of Hindu mysticism; in his later years he would list Eliot's poem along with the *Bhagavad-Gita* among the ten books that had shaped his philosophy of life. He realized during his sophomore year, 1923—looking to essences again—that in chemistry he had chosen the wrong major; he submitted himself to the distinguished physicist Percy Bridgman and switched to physics. Alfred North Whitehead arrived at Harvard the same year, and Oppenheimer submitted also to him. Nobel laureate Hans Bethe, who reported to Oppenheimer at Los Alamos and admired him warmly, exhumed the connection. Oppenheimer "worked at physics," Bethe told a biographer, "mainly because he found physics the best way to do philosophy." He graduated in three years, *summa cum laude* and first in his class, with the highest grade average Harvard ever recorded, but not yet, in his own severe judgment, a human being. Harvard, he would say, was "the most exciting time I've ever had in my life. I really had a chance to learn. I loved it. I almost came alive." Noting the prodigious intake, Bridgman warned him not to consider himself a physicist until he'd done original work. He faced that sentence next.

At the Cavendish, Cambridge University's celebrated laboratory, he struggled for the first time to do physics originally and alone. Before he succeeded, the self-doubt the effort exposed almost destroyed him. "My feeling about myself," he said of this period, "was always one of extreme discontent." A Cambridge friend remembered finding him groaning, rolling on the floor. He went into treatment with a London psychiatrist. "I was on the point of bumping myself off. This was chronic." The psychiatrist

Ca. 1909

diagnosed dementia praecox—schizophrenia—and refused to continue treatment. Oppenheimer went off to Corsica on spring holiday with friends, to whom he announced that his ideal man would be widely talented but would look at the world with a "tear-stained countenance."

Something happened on Corsica to change his mind, something he would later reveal only in hints: he met a woman, probably a married woman, and learned the certification of love. He returned to Corsica for the summer. "A great thing in my life," he told biographer Nuel Pharr Davis, "a great and lasting part of it. . . . You can't dig it out. What you need to know is that it was not a mere love affair, not a love affair at all, but love." Love affair or love, it persisted only in correspondence or memory. During the Corsica summer, Oppenheimer read Proust's *Remembrance of Things Past* in its entirety, and mingling the two Corsica experiences in recollection a decade later, he told his Berkeley friend Haakon Chevalier that reading Proust had been "one of the great experiences in his life." To Chevalier he quoted from Proust a telling passage: "Perhaps she would not have considered evil to be so rare . . . had she been able to discern in herself, as in everyone, that indifference to the sufferings one causes, an indifference which, whatever other names one may give it, is the terrible and permanent form of cruelty."

The woman may have been unknowingly indifferent to his sufferings, but something in the relationship set Oppenheimer's "dementia praecox" healing. Entrained for doctoral study at the University of Göttingen in the autumn of 1926, with two of his papers accepted for publication in the *Proceedings of the Cambridge Philosophical Society*, he had at last begun to come alive as a physicist and a man.

Göttingen, the German university where the most advanced physics of the day, quantum mechanics, took form—a cathedral of sorts, the work of many hands—was triumph again, not apprenticeship this time but solid achievement. Oppenheimer's special contribution, appropriate to the sweep of his mind, was to extend quantum theory beyond its narrow initial ground.

Oppenheimer's Ph.D. thesis, "On the Quantum Theory of Continuous Spectra," composed in German, appeared in the *Zeitschrift für Physik* in 1927. Max Born, his teacher, marked it "with distinction"; and, added to the sixteen papers he published between 1926 and 1929, it established for him an international reputation. He came home to lecture at Harvard and Caltech—shouting "Quantize it! Quantize it!" to startled students—then returned to Europe to study with Paul Ehrenfest and Wolfgang Pauli at Leiden and Zurich. At Göttingen he had mastered Italian well enough in one month's study to read Dante; at Leiden he lectured in Dutch six weeks after he arrived. Pauli found his thinking slack—"Pauli once remarked to me," writes physicist I. I. Rabi, a Nobel laureate and Oppenheimer's staunch defender at the 1954 security hearings, "that Oppenheimer seemed to treat physics as an avocation and psychoanalysis as a vocation"—and fiercely tightened him up. The price of the mental thumbscrewing was tuberculosis, which Oppenheimer dried out that summer, 1929, at Perro Caliente, his New Mexican ranch. Returning to Berkeley in the fall, he was prepared to found there and at Caltech a school of theoretical physics, whose international reputation would eventually rival Göttingen's.

After 1929 and through the decade of the 1930's, a decade marked by his mother's and father's deaths—another lading of grief, another accounting of manhood—Oppenheimer dug harder for originality. He formulated the Dirac theory, an extension of quantum mechanics to include the theory of relativity, as a field theory, and was the first to predict the antiproton (his paper on this, like most of his later papers, was coauthored). He formulated the Tunnel Effect, the principle upon which the tunnel diode of electronics is based. He enlarged theoretical understanding of cosmic rays. Modeling the imploding collapse of dying suns, he predicted the neutron star—the pulsar, discovered in the 1960's, is one such structure—and the black hole. He was primarily interested in particle physics—"I never found nuclear physics so beautiful," he said—but working with Ernest O. Lawrence and his cyclotrons at Berkeley, he became an expert on nuclear matters as well. By 1945 he had published a total of sixty-six papers; after the war, particle physics would dominate American physical studies, a lasting tribute to his influence on the American school.

Without question, Oppenheimer's intelligence exceeded that of any of his

Ca. 1914

peers—"I was never in the same class with him," I. I. Rabi remarked—but despite the breadth of his contribution, he reined back from work historically unique. Writing for the 1967 Oppenheimer Memorial Session of the American Physical Society, Rabi attempted to explain the hesitation:

"Oppenheimer understood the whole structure of physics with extraordinary clarity, and not only the structure, but the interactions between the different elements. Hardly any branch of physics was foreign to him. As well as theoretical physics, he also had a vast knowledge of experimental results and methods at his fingertips and would continually amaze experimenters by his great knowledge of their own subject—in some respects exceeding their own, especially in fields of great current interest. . . .

"One often wonders why men of Oppenheimer's gifts do not discover everything worth discovering. . . . [I]t seems to me that in some respects Oppenheimer was overeducated in those fields which lie outside the scientific tradition, such as his interest in religion, in the Hindu religion in particular, which resulted in a feeling for the mystery of the universe that surrounded him almost like a fog. He saw physics clearly, looking toward what had already been done, but at the border he tended to feel that there was much more of the mysterious and novel than there actually was. . . . Some may call it a lack of faith, but in my opinion it was more a turning away from the hard, crude methods of theoretical physics into a mystical realm of broad intuition."

And closing his tribute, Rabi netted the essential man in a qualified benediction. "In Oppenheimer," he wrote, "the element of earthiness was feeble."

Haakon Chevalier, Oppenheimer's Berkeley pal in the later years of the Depression, a professor of French and dallier with Communism whose relations with Oppenheimer would be ground to Paris green at security-hearing time, inhaled the fog of sanctification and supplied the most concise physical description the record contains:

"[Oppenheimer] was tall, nervous and intent, and he moved with an odd gait, a kind of jog, with a great deal of swinging of his limbs, his head always a little to one side, one shoulder higher than the other. But it was the head that was most striking: the halo of whispy black curly hair, the fine, sharp nose, and especially the eyes, surprisingly blue, having a strange depth and intensity, and yet expressive of a candor that was altogether disarming. He looked like a young Einstein, and at the same time like an overgrown choir boy."

Oppenheimer's students, in those infatuate prewar days, idolized him even to aping his mannerisms, moving with odd gaits all over Berkeley. Chevalier idolized him too, and so fails to mention the self-inflicted stigmata: the forced insomnia, the ravaged teeth, the extreme emaciation (Oppenheimer, six feet tall, never in his life weighed more than 130 pounds, and in times of exceptional stress would tighten to a cadaverous 113), the caustic martinis thrown on a tender stomach, the chains of smoke wheezed through tubercular lungs.

These were the years of the left-wing movement in America, when Communism was openly discussed and openly avowed on college campuses everywhere. Walking with Oppenheimer in San Francisco one day in 1930, Ernest Lawrence discovered he had not yet heard of the Wall Street Crash. The benevolent mentor, who shared with his students the coauthorship of signal papers and supplemented their diets at the best restaurants in town, learned to his indignation that all his influence could not lever them into nonexistent teaching jobs; and apprehending that, quick study that he was, he apprehended the revolutionary forces the Depression set loose.

The plight of his students exposed Oppenheimer to social injustice, peeled back the insulation of his wealth; the desperation of his German aunt and cousins to escape to America from the eugenic hallucinations of the Nazis, an escape that in 1937 he underwrote, alerted him to fascism. Both intercessions moved him leftward, but the private reason he joined the fringes of the Communist movement in Berkeley was probably emotional adaptation to the rebellious standards of a woman he loved and hoped to salvage, Jean Tatlock, the lithe, chiaroscuro daughter of an anti-Semite Berkeley medievalist. Though he never, like her, joined the party, finding its dialectics less rigorous than his taste, he espoused her cause, read Engels and Feuerbach and all of Marx, attended meetings, tithed. What he earned in return from Jean Tatlock—as, more obscurely, from the woman in Corsica before—was passionate acceptance, and with that acceptance a bolder emotional commitment to humanity, including his own. The woman he married for life in 1940, Katherine Puening, Kitty, who had lost a heroic Communist husband, a Dartmouth man, on the practice battlefields of revolutionary Spain, who dedicated herself now to nurturing and supporting him, sealed that commitment.

Oppenheimer pilgrimaged to the women in his life afflicted with more than diffidence, afflicted with something worse than the stylish Harvard *Weltschmerz* his detractors thought they saw (his enemies caught its hot scent, though they inverted it and imagined him Machiavellian at least, if not actually diabolic): afflicted with a pathological disgust with himself and a nearly pathological horror of the world. Only once, on the record, did he emerge from stoic privacy to reveal the depth of that disgust—after years of marital devotion had sweetened it, and for an important cause. "Up to now, and even more in the days of my almost infinitely prolonged adolescence," he told a group of culturally distinguished peers he'd assembled to discuss the possibility of peace, "I hardly took an action, hardly did anything, or failed to do anything, whether it was a paper on physics, or a lecture, or how I read a book, how I talked to a friend, how I loved, that did not arouse in me a very great sense of revulsion and of wrong." Which is to say more than that his standards were impossibly high: which is to say that he perceived himself worse than a failure, perceived himself a thing loathsome before the world. He realized to his survival, if not his salvation, that the women in his life saw him otherwise:

"It turned out to be impossible . . . for me to live with anybody else, without understanding that what I saw was only one part of the truth . . . and in an attempt to break out and be a reasonable man, I had to realize that my own worries about what I did were valid and were important, but that they were not the whole story, that there must be a complementary way of looking at them, because other people did not see them as I did. And I needed what they saw, needed them."

He proffered his thanks subtly, but in scale with his gratitude. In the final days of the Manhattan Project, with Jean Tatlock recently dead by her own hand, he restored himself rereading John Donne's *Holy Sonnets*. When an assistant requested a code name for the first bomb test, to be conducted on a ghastly stretch of southern New Mexico desert the conquistadors had named the *Jornada del Muerto*, the Journey of Death, he thought of the rapt sonnet that begins, "Batter my heart, three-personed God," and coded the test "Trinity." He had more than one trinity in mind, but one, an important one, may have been Corsica, Jean Tatlock, and Kitty Oppenheimer. His trinity of women had given him a bearable life on earth; he gave them, in return, the first crude man-made star, a weapon so terrifying that it might, in time, force peace upon the world.

The hope of peace in terror was one of the reasons he agreed to direct the building of the bomb. Its potential for monumental effect had caught his attention from the beginning. When Niels Bohr, the great Danish physicist who may have been the man he most deeply admired, brought the news of nuclear fission to America on January 26, 1939, Oppenheimer's response must have seemed incongruous to those who could not fathom his contrarieties: "On the very day he received the news of fission," writes biographer Denise Royal, "Oppenheimer started making rough calculations on the critical mass necessary to bring about an explosion." He refined his calculations with Edward Teller, Robert Serber, and Hans Bethe, among others, at Berkeley, through 1941. A critical mass of U-235, they decided, would form an eight-inch sphere; they also decided that the odds of that mass starting a fusion reaction in the air's nitrogen or the ocean's deuterium and burning up the earth were no more than three in a million, long odds but heady eschatology for physicists then obscure.

Appointed Coordinator of Rapid Rupture, a title that delighted him, by the bomb committee that Franklin Roosevelt had established to shepherd nuclear weapons research, Oppenheimer surveyed the work of bomb design being conducted at small laboratories scattered across the United States, none of them allowed to talk to each other, and proposed that the separate projects be assembled in one place under one director. Whoever would be that director would have to deal with Brigadier General Leslie R. Groves, the overweight Corps of Engineers talent who had built the Pentagon in record time and who

1925

was now the head of the Manhattan Project—a blustering, difficult man. Oppenheimer was not the obvious choice. Groves and others believed the director should be a Nobel laureate; Army Counter-Intelligence was adamant that he should be politically safe; Oppenheimer was neither. In 1942, despite his lack of administrative qualification, Oppenheimer won Groves's nod—"by default," he said later, but also by coaching Groves on physics, by serving, as biographer Nuel Pharr Davis puts it, as an "idiot savant," and by sparing the general's ego when he asked stupid questions as Oppenheimer never spared his students'. To appoint Oppenheimer, Groves had to override his security staff's objections; he did, and he said later he never doubted that Oppenheimer was loyal, however pink his past. Groves's staff had no such confidence, and shadowed, bugged, and interrogated the bomb director throughout the war. It was during those wartime interrogations that Oppenheimer reported— painfully or gratuitously: the fading transcripts do not indicate which—on the political activities of some of his friends.

Oppenheimer located the bomb lab in his beloved New Mexico, across the Rio Grande from Perro Caliente, on a 7,200-foot mesa, commandeering a rugged boys' school for the base of established buildings it supplied. He led the lab, Los Alamos, with a skill so dazzling—inspiring and coordinating the work of a thousand men and women from a dozen different countries, many of whom were prima donnas, lone wolves, iconoclasts—that its story is worn to legend now. "Here at Los Alamos," one hardheaded British physicist said afterward, "I found a spirit of Athens, of Plato, of an ideal Republic." Others called those years of backbreaking labor on a remote mesa—years spent locked behind high barbed-wire fences living in flimsy barracks modified to apartments with pasteboard partitions and filthy coal-burning stoves, years deflected to technology while creative physics stalled—"the best years of our lives." All but a few of those who lived them agreed that Oppenheimer—"Oppie," they called him, resurrecting the affectionate diminutive Leiden had bestowed— made them so. Oppie's whistle blew at seven in the morning and they came out cheering to work eighteen-hour days building weapons of mass destruction. "I believe," said Enrico Fermi incredulously, come down one day from atomic pile-building in Chicago, "your people actually *want* to make a bomb." They did, because Oppie did.

Why he did he never directly explained. It is perhaps his deepest mystery. Certainly he despised the Nazis for what they had done to physics and physicists and to political and intellectual freedom; from his aunt and cousins he knew the Nazi pogroms at close second hand. George F. Kennan, his neighbor in Princeton during the postwar years, when Oppenheimer directed the Institute for Advanced Study, perceived another level of it. He discerned in Oppenheimer, he told journalist Philip M. Stern, "a deep yearning for . . . friendship, for companionship, for the warmth and richness of human communication. The arrogance which to many appeared to be a part of his personality masked in reality an overpowering desire to bestow and to receive affection. Neither circumstances nor at times the asperities of his own temperament permitted the gratification of this need in a measure remotely approaching its intensity; and in this too lay a portion of that strong element of tragedy which all who knew him sensed . . . in his situation."

Early 1940's

Humanly enough, Oppenheimer wanted desperately to be liked, admired, adulated, even loved, and building the ultimate weapon, serving his country at the extreme limit of his special talent for physics and for the charismatic direction of difficult, talented men, was a way to achieve that acclaim, particularly since he already understood that at thirty-eight his best years as a theoretical physicist were behind him and had left him first-rate but not first-rank in the scientific annals of the age.

Niels Bohr helped him see at Los Alamos what the highest officials of the United States government failed at first to comprehend: that nuclear weapons would make world war suicidal and therefore obsolete. "First of all," Oppenheimer wrote in 1964, "[Bohr] was clear that if it worked, this development would bring an enormous change in the situation of the world, and of war. . . . When he came to Los Alamos, his first serious question was, 'Is it really big enough?' I do not know whether it was; it did finally get to be." And, further: "Bohr at Los Alamos was marvelous. He took a very lively technical interest. But his real function, I think for almost all of us, was not the technical one. He made the enterprise seem hopeful, when many were not free of misgiving. Bohr spoke with contempt of Hitler, who with a few hundred tanks and planes had tried to enslave Europe for a millennium. His own high hope that the outcome would be good, that the objectivity, the cooperation of the sciences would play a helpful part, we all wanted to believe."

Oppenheimer carried these considerations into his interior depths, measuring them against the only moral technical manual he seriously credited, the *Bhagavad-Gita*. "It is the most beautiful philosophical song existing in any known tongue," he said once of that 700-stanzaed devotional poem interpolated into the great Aryan epic *Mahabharata* at about the same time that Greece was declining from its golden age. He had discovered it at Harvard; at Berkeley he had learned Sanskrit from the scholar Arthur Ryder to set himself closer to the original text; a worn pink copy of the *Gita* thereafter occupied an honored place on the bookshelf closest to his desk, for the same reason that divers keep a decompression table near at hand.

There are meanings enough for a lifetime in the *Gita*, dramatized as a dialogue between a warrior prince named Arjuna and Krishna, the principal avatar of Vishnu (and Vishnu the third member of the Hindu godhead with Brahma and Shiva—a trinity again). In the moments before a major battle, seeing his teachers and kinsmen and friends opposed to him on the battlefield, Arjuna refuses to fight. Through dialogue, Krishna justifies the battle to the prince. He has a duty to his class, Krishna argues; discipline will free him from guilt in the spirit of sacrifice; and anyway, the Supreme Lord is everywhere, in the slayer and the slain:

> Today behold the whole world
> All things that move or do not move
> And whatever else you wish to see.
> They stand as one within my body.

1945

Perverted, that argument would justify a Charles Manson in casual, random murder, but though Oppenheimer personally bore his share of guilt—"Mr. President," he told an impatient Harry Truman in 1947, "I feel I have blood on my hands"—he had something else, something far less insanely subjective, in mind: the *inevitability* of discovery, the certainty that having found fission, and after it fusion, some nation somewhere would put it to terrible use. "It is a profound and necessary truth," he told a Canadian audience in 1962, "that the deep things in science are not found because they are useful; they are found because it was possible to find them." He wanted the United States to find them first, because he believed—who can say erroneously?—that it was the one country capable of building nuclear weapons that might in the fullness of time arrange to forestall their use.

But first he wanted the bombs used, to force the changes Bohr anticipated. The record leaves no doubt that he acquiesced to the bombing of Japanese cities. He attended the meetings where the recommendation to use the bombs against Japanese civilians was formulated; he was the most qualified technical adviser there; and in that vital capacity he argued against a bloodless demonstration on the specious technical grounds that the bomb used in such a demonstration might be a dud, though he knew to virtual certainty that it would not. He would soon send the uranium bomb, Little Boy, ahead untested to Tinian for the Hiroshima drop, and he tested Fat Man at Trinity and knew its lethal twin would work. He was forthright enough after the war. "I am very glad that the bomb was not kept secret," he said in one of his lectures. The understatement is typical, is even mocking: Oppenheimer meant he was glad the bomb was used, its destructive force horribly and indelibly demonstrated. "I am glad," he went on, "that all of us knew, as a few of us already did, what was up and what readjustments in human life and in political institutions would be called for."

And so, in that first man-made dawn, when the nest of the Chinese boxes that was not Thor or Jesu or The Liberator but Fat Man, the plutonium bomb—spheres within spheres contained within a black duralumin shell studded with detonators—collapsed upon itself like a dying sun and blew Oppenheimer's serenely elegant physics out to plague the world, he understood through the visionary extremity of his exhaustion that Krishna had once again made his point. He thought, he said later, of a stanza and a line from the *Gita* that described the twin and complementary qualities of the godhead that was the bomb, of the bomb that was less than, but part of, the godhead:

> If the radiance of a thousand suns
> were to burst into the sky,
> that would be like
> the splendor of the Mighty One—

And as the thunder rolled east and west across the *Jornada del Muerto*, echoing from the fastness of mountains:

> I am become Death, the shatterer of worlds.

Krishna; the fiery universe of stars and neutron stars and black holes and cosmic rays; the particles that were also waves and the waves that were also particles, but never, to the possibility of human measurement, both at once; the mc^2 that is also E: these were death, and worlds were shattered; these were splendor, and worlds radiated light; and these were men and women contending below; these were the truth that must inevitably be found because it was possible to find it; and these were as well the hope of no more wars. Between death and splendor, one suspects, he thought the contest no better than an even match.

He did his best, in the years after the war, to transmute the threat of shattering nuclear annihilation into a radiant cause for peace. It was, paradoxically, that effort—there are reversals in Robert Oppenheimer's life as drastic as any in *Oedipus*—that led to his public humiliation, that led President Eisenhower to throw up a "blank wall" between him and the official secrets that he carried in his head, that led the Eisenhower government, pushed by men like Joseph McCarthy and the imperious Lewis Strauss, men like Richard Nixon (he was there too, giving "assurances" to the McCarthy crowd that "the Oppenheimer case" "would be gone into in detail"), to convene a prosecutorial hearing and deprive him of his security clearance on the grounds, in his case the absurd grounds, that his character was dangerously marred by "fundamental defects." That story is legend too, but documents declassified within the past year have chiseled some of its ambiguities away.

With Niels Bohr's proposals much in mind, Oppenheimer worked with a government committee that included David Lilienthal and Dean Acheson to formulate the Baruch Plan of 1946 that proposed to internationalize atomic energy. Whether or not it was offered in good faith—Oppenheimer and others vehemently insisted it was—the Soviet Union rejected it, refusing to give up secrecy for mutual protection from nuclear war, and Oppenheimer consigned the Soviet Union to the same midden he reserved in his mind for the Third Reich. But in 1949 he and the other members of the Atomic Energy Commission's General Advisory Committee—tough men like Enrico Fermi, I. I. Rabi, James B. Conant—saw another opportunity, one they rated at no better than even odds: that if the United States held off building fusion weapons, thermonuclear weapons, hydrogen bombs, then so might the Soviets.

Stated so baldly, the idea sounds ridiculously naive, but the GAC was anything but naive. The hydrogen bomb that in 1949 the members of that committee, all scientists, thought they might, within five years, be able to build—they called it the "Super"—would not have been Edward Teller's and Stanislaw Ulam's later true thermonuclear weapon, the weapon Oppenheimer would call "technically sweet," but a booster device, a very large fission bomb with a small thermonuclear component. It would not generate an explosive force equivalent to the combined force of a number of fission bombs containing the same amount of plutonium. Oppenheimer, among others, feared that an all-out push for the Super would therefore be cheap and dangerous defense, and believed the United States would be better off enlarging and diversifying its fission arsenal with the limited uranium and plutonium then being produced.

Some of the members of the GAC believed that building the Super was morally wrong, because it was entirely a strategic weapon, intended to fry civilians a city at a time; but all the members of the GAC believed that building it was militarily wrong, that diversification of the fission arsenal was the better defense. Military men, and most notably the generals of the Strategic Air Command, who had a monopoly on nuclear weapons at that point within the American military and wanted to keep it, angrily disagreed. But the most conservative scenario that anyone has since been able to devise—a recent reconstruction is Herbert York's in *Scientific American*, founded on the GAC's newly declassified minutes—indicates that Oppenheimer and the GAC were right, that even if the United States had not built the hydrogen bomb first, even if it had waited until after the Soviets tested theirs, the balance of terror would not have been shifted by so much as an inch, because the United States would have had, in fission weapons, more than an equivalency, and could quickly have added thermonuclear weapons to its arsenal.

Despite the GAC's considered recommendation, President Truman, on January 31, 1950, ordered a crash program to build hydrogen bombs. If he underestimated Soviet science—he told Oppenheimer, before the first Soviet nuclear test in 1949, that the Russians could never make the bomb—he understood politics, and knew that no administration that unilaterally restrained itself from reaching for military superiority would long survive.

The other GAC members accepted the inevitable. Oppenheimer did not. He continued to battle for nuclear diversification, and for good measure he threw in continental defense, which the Air Force thought impossible. And as, with Bohr, he had anticipated the revolutionary changes in the nature of war that atomic weapons would bring, so also he anticipated the nuclear stalemate. And announcing that paradox, declaring the futility of the arms race, was viewed as more than error: it was nothing less than heresy.

"The answer to fear," Oppenheimer told Eleanor Roosevelt on her national radio program twelve days after Truman bluntly overruled the GAC, "cannot always lie in the dissipation of the causes of fear; sometimes it lies in courage." Courageously, in 1953, he took his argument to the makers of government policy and then to the open world, delivering to the Council on Foreign Affairs and then publishing in *Foreign Affairs* a statement that is distinguished from all his other published statements by its passion, its anger, and its cold contempt for those who behind walls of secrecy would drag the United States into military danger and the world into an arms race that no nation could conceivably win. It was this statement that condemned him. Its essence is distilled in one ironic central paragraph:

"The very least we can say is that, looking ten years ahead, it is likely to be small comfort that the Soviet Union is four years behind us [it was less than nine months], and small comfort that they are only about half as big [industrially] as we are. The very least we can conclude is that our twenty-thousandth bomb, useful as it may be in filling the vast munitions pipelines of a great war, will not in any deep strategic sense offset their two-thousandth."

And further to clinch the argument:

"We may anticipate a state of affairs in which two Great Powers will each be in a position to put an end to the civilization and life of the other, though not without risking its own. We may be likened to two scorpions in a bottle, each capable of killing the other, but only at the risk of his own life."

And finally, indignantly and properly contemptuous of militarists so glory bound that they could not distinguish between glory and nuclear holocaust:

"We need to be clear that there will not be many great atomic wars for us, nor for our institutions. It is important that there not be one."

The vivid desert metaphor, the scorpions in a bottle, applied to the reality of nuclear stalemate within Oppenheimer's lifetime, and the policies he espoused of tactical and strategic flexibility, of early warning and continental defense, of phased disarmament, are official policy now.

But "massive retaliation" was official policy under John Foster Dulles and Dwight Eisenhower, a bigger bang for the buck, and in 1954 Oppenheimer was summoned, and scourged, and thrown down from government and the gates locked behind. Atomic Energy Commission chairman Lewis Strauss, a man whom Oppenheimer had publicly ridiculed at congressional hearings on atomic secrecy a few years before, was immediately responsible for the security review "In the Matter of J. Robert Oppenheimer" convened in a jerrybuilt World War II building in Washington in March and April of 1954. But behind him were more shadowy figures, the enraged and vengeful generals of the Strategic Air Command first of all.

The security hearing was not a hearing at all but a purge, a trial conducted without the protection of courtroom procedures and in violation of all the usual

1954

rules of evidence. The AEC had cleared Oppenheimer of his left-wing escapades and his single wartime indiscretion—temporarily refusing to give Army Counter-Intelligence the name of a man who reported to him a Soviet spying probe (the man was his friend Haakon Chevalier)—in 1947. All the old charges were raked up again, and countered by a parade of distinguished witnesses who testified to Oppenheimer's loyalty, men such as I. I. Rabi, Hans Bethe, Vannevar Bush, James B. Conant, and even, though more ambiguously, General Leslie R. Groves. But most of the interminable spring days were devoted to Oppenheimer's opposition to the H-bomb, an opposition the entire GAC had shared, and the witnesses who condemned that opposition, Edward Teller the star among them, were unsparing in voicing their suspicions of him. Oppenheimer defended himself numbly and inadequately, shaken by the viciousness of the attack. When the hearings were finished, not even Lewis Strauss could find solid evidence of security violations. He lifted Oppenheimer's top-secret "Q" clearance just the same.

No one who objectively studies the record today, two decades later, can come away with any doubt of Oppenheimer's innocence from wrongdoing except the political wrongdoing of disagreeing on government policy. For that disagreement, in a nation constitutionally pledged to freedom of speech, he was officially destroyed. "Oppenheimer's life," writes Nuel Pharr Davis angrily, "can stand inspection down to the last senseless detail. One must, finally, put all this damned nonsense, to use Oppenheimer's term for the hearings, into its proper, dismally small perspective in order to gain any comprehension of Oppenheimer as a scientist, American, or human being."

The "damned nonsense" was dismally small, but its effects were not. Oppenheimer went home to Princeton visibly aged. He had turned fifty during the hearings; a former student who saw him afterward in Princeton remarked that he had always looked younger than his years, but now looked older. "Much of his previous spirit and liveliness had left him," Hans Bethe sadly confirmed. He never complained of it, no more than he had complained of the bullying incident at Camp Koenig thirty-six years before. "I think of this as a major accident," he told an interviewer,"—much like a train wreck or the collapse of a building. It has no relation or connection with my life. I just happened to be there." It may have been a major accident for the United States as well, because it deprived the nation of the experience, the intelligence, and the prescience of one of its most able sons.

He lived the last decade of his life in a lonely isolation that he also never complained of and that the honors that came to him did not alleviate. He had been appointed director of the Institute for Advanced Study in 1946; he kept the position until a year before his death, and also assumed Einstein's old post as senior professor of physics. He was called to speak to the world from Paris, from South America, from England and Japan, and finally from within the United States. John Kennedy invited him to dine at the White House with forty-nine Nobel laureates in 1961, and planned to award him the Enrico Fermi Award, the AEC's highest honor, on December 2, 1963; Lyndon Johnson, in a time of mourning, made the presentation to Oppenheimer in the White House Cabinet Room—a medal, and $50,000 to take home, from an agency that still denied him clearance as a security risk.

He retired from the institute in 1966, when illness weakened him. On his last visit to the institute, writes the physicist Abraham Pais, "He came to participate in a discussion on the selection of the young physicists who would be members of the Institute during the coming academic year. He knew he would not be there to greet them."

Every thoughtful human being projects, somewhere within himself, a vision of utopia, a vision usually reconstructed from an imagined golden age. That golden age is frequently childhood, but Oppenheimer's spare childhood would not serve; instead he found his golden age at Göttingen, and constructed his utopia from the materials there at hand. Because Göttingen was a community of scientists, Oppenheimer's utopia is more convoluted, and more tragic, than most. It considers not only the possibility of peace and communion among men but also the certainty that the larger universe is fatally inanimate, in basic ways opaque, and ultimately destructive of all human pretension, even the necessary pretension of hope.

Despite the baleful finalities, his vision was guardedly optimistic and far from Faustian. He thought that the community of scientists throughout the world, a community protected from too grievous error by the necessary and inherent openness of its work, might serve as a modest model for a peaceful, open world. Proposing such a model, he cautioned humility:

"This is a world in which each of us, knowing his limitations, knowing the evils of superficiality and the terrors of fatigue, will have to cling to what is close to him, to what he knows, to what he can do, to his friends and his tradition and his love, lest he be dissolved in a universal confusion and know nothing and love nothing. It is at the same time a world in which none of us can find hieratic prescription or general sanction for any ignorance, any insensitivity, any indifference. When a friend tells us of a new discovery we may not understand, we may not be able to listen without jeopardizing the work that is ours and closer to us; but we cannot find in a book or canon—and we should not seek—grounds for hallowing our ignorance. If a man tells us that he sees differently than we, or that he finds beautiful what we find ugly, we may have to leave the room, from fatigue or trouble; but that is our weakness and our default. If we must live with a perpetual sense that the world and the men in it are greater than we and too much for us, let it be the measure of our virtue that we know this and seek no comfort. Above all, let us not proclaim that the limits of our powers correspond to some special wisdom in our choice of life, of learning, or of beauty."

Yet he knew the futility of words to change the world. He believed in Bohr's principle of complementarity; he believed there are manifold ways of observation and manifold forms of action; he did not content himself with words. Out of physics, in concert with others from that community of scientists that was his model for utopia, he drew a simple and fundamental fact, that matter is only another form of energy and may be converted back to energy at will: that $E = mc^2$. With that incontrovertible certainty, he made his argument secure, and assembled the bomb for us as a puzzle, a puzzle as Gordian and tangled as he was himself, knowing, this mystical man, that we would either learn in time to unravel it or explosively abrogate our claim to mastery of the earth.

J. Robert Oppenheimer died on February 18, 1967, at the age of sixty-two. His ashes were scattered on the ocean off the Virgin Islands—the ocean with its vast reserves of nuclear fuel, the ocean with its depths. Among his last published words were these: "Science is not everything, but science is very beautiful." And, the child and the man within the scientist: "No one should say there is no hope."

Since he was buried in the sea, no epitaph marks his grave. A stanza from the *Bhagavad-Gita* might serve, though he would be the first to say it is not the whole story, is only one of several complementary and mutually exclusive points of view. He deserves it, if anyone among those who devised the machinery of nuclear holocaust does, in mitigation of the guilt he carried to his death for serving as loyally and as intelligently as he knew:

> But he who is without thought of "I,"
> Whose understanding is pure
> Even though he should slay whole worlds
> He does not slay, nor is he bound.

Richard Rhodes is a journalist and novelist with a deep interest in history. His new novel, Holy Secrets, *is to be published by Doubleday in January, 1978. He is currently at work on another novel,* Fissions, *centered on nuclear scientists.*

Oppenheimer, photographed in June, 1966, eight months before his death

PAGES 72, 73, 74, AND 77: OPPENHEIMER MEMORIAL COMMITTEE. PAGE 76: HARVARD UNIVERSITY ARCHIVES. PAGE 78: WIDE WORLD. PAGE 80: ALFRED EISENSTAEDT. *Life* MAGAZINE © TIME, INC. PAGE 83: RANDALL HAGADORN

By His Excellency

Benjamin Fletcher, Captain General and Governor in Chief of Their Majesties Province of *New-York*, Province of *Pennsilvania*, Country of *New-Castle*, and the Territories and Tracts of Land depending thereon in *America*, and Vice-Admiral of the same.

A PROCLAMATION

Province of New-York, *ss.*

WHereas I have received Information, That the *French* have designed an Attempt upon this City and Province, the Prevention whereof is not only the Interest and Duty of all their Majesties Subjects inhabiting and residing within the same, but of the Outmost Consequence to all the *English* Plantations in *America*. And in regard the Defence of this City is the Safety of the whole Province, and not to be maintained without considerable Numbers of Men to be drawn from all parts hither, to form such a Body as may be capable to Resist the Force of the Enemy, Which Numbers of Men will not be able to subsist in this Place without Considerable Stores of Provisions, I have therefore thought fit, by and with the Advice and Consent of Their Majesties Council, to Prohibit and Forbid the Exportation of any Provisions from this Province. And I do hereby strictly Charge and Require all and every Their Majesties Subjects in this Province, That they do not Export from this Province any Flower, Bread, Beef or Pork, until further Order, as they will answer the contrary hereof at their Peril.

Given at Fort William Henry *the* 19th *Day of* August, 1693. *Anno; Regni Regis & Regina Gulielmi & Marie Anglie, &c. quinto.*

Ben. Fletcher.

God Save King William & Queen Mary.

Printed and Sold by William Bradford, *Printer to Their Majesties, King* William *and* Queen Mary *at the City of* New-York, 1693.

When New York Feared the French

In 1693 the people of New York had more to worry about than a fiscal crisis, as the newly revealed documents on these pages attest. The British colonies were in the fourth year of King William's War—a bloody struggle that had already seen fierce wilderness fighting and the savage destruction of Schenectady by the French and their Algonquian allies. Now New Yorkers feared that a daring blow was to be aimed against Manhattan. Benjamin Fletcher, the royal governor, called upon the citizenry to rally to the colony's defense, store up provisions, and pray for the success of English arms. The expected assault never materialized, but the colony remained jittery until the Peace of Ryswick officially ended hostilities between England and France in 1697.

These three documents, which illuminate that early moment of New York's history, are part of an extraordinary collection of some of the first materials ever printed in that colony. They have just been acquired by the New-York Historical Society and are the work of William Bradford, the first printer in the colony of New York. Bradford, inspired by the teachings of George Fox, left England to join the Quakers in Pennsylvania in 1685. In his eight years there he became embroiled in so many civil and religious disputes that, when Governor Fletcher called him to New York, his presses and paper had been confiscated and he was languishing in jail. He managed the move, however, and served as New York's official printer until 1742, ten years before his death. His output included New York's first paper currency (1709), the first American *Book of Common Prayer* (1710), and New York's first newspaper, the *New-York Gazette* (1725). But surviving examples of the documents he printed are rare, and the total of eleven that the New-York Historical Society has acquired constitute a unique find indeed.

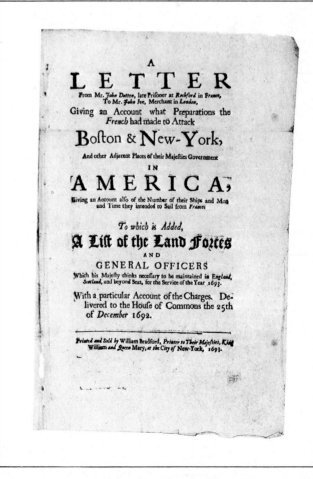

THE LOST BATTALION
by Joe McCarthy

Above is Major Charles Whittlesey, the scholarly soldier whose leadership under fire won him the Congressional Medal of Honor. His finest hour is depicted on the preceding page: the bespectacled major (center) reads the enemy demand for surrender brought through his lines by a blindfolded German soldier. (Actually the messenger was an American who had been captured by the Germans.) Though his battered command was surrounded, Whittlesey refused even to reply. The painting was made by Frank E. Schoonover for Ladies' Home Journal, *February, 1919.*

ABOVE: U.S. SIGNAL CORPS, NATIONAL ARCHIVES
PRECEDING PAGE: CORTLANDT SCHOONOVER AND THE
DELAWARE NATIONAL GUARD

In the early fall of 1918 five hundred American infantrymen were cut off from their regiment and surrounded by Germans during five days of fighting in the Argonne Forest. Though they would be forever remembered as the Lost Battalion, they were not really a battalion and they were never lost. "We knew exactly where we were," one of them said later. "So did the Germans." The only nearby Americans uncertain about the location of the trapped band of riflemen and machine gunners were their own division's artillery officers, who bombarded them with heavy shellfire for two terrifying hours during the second day of the siege.

The encircled group of doughboys, about 550 men, were survivors from four battalions of the New York Seventy-seventh Division's infantry that had been hard hit during the previous week's opening drive of the big American offensive against the fortified German lines between the Argonne Forest and the Meuse River. This was to be General John J. Pershing's all-out effort to show the world that his United States First Army could win the war before Christmas by breaking through a sector of the Western Front that the enemy had held firmly for four years. Pershing had warned his corps and division commanders that he wanted no alibis, no slowdowns in the planned advance.

The big push started on the morning of September 26 after a 24-hour artillery bombardment dropped forty thousand tons of explosives on the German lines—more shells than all of the cannon ammunition fired by the Union Army in the Civil War. The Seventy-seventh Division, in the thickest section of the Argonne Forest on the far left flank of Pershing's forces, moved ahead rapidly during the first day's advance, assaulting one enemy pavilion after another. The German pavilions, built in depth throughout the forest, were elaborately equipped blockhouses with ground-level concrete roofs twenty feet thick. Breaking into some of these hurriedly deserted fortifications, the astonished Americans found bathtubs with hot and cold running water, bowling alleys and billiard tables, pantries well stocked with wine and meat, electric power plants, and underground dormitories with comfortable bunks for fifty enlisted men. The Germans, undisturbed in the securely protected Argonne Forest for four years, had been living well.

After the encouraging first day's advance of about four to six miles—a considerable distance in the almost stationary combat of World War I—the American attack stalled, not only in the

Argonne, but all along the First Army's front eastward to the Meuse. "The assault of 26 September," Pershing wrote later, "surprised the Germans and disrupted their defense, but this situation was only momentary. From that day on the fighting was probably unsurpassed during the World War for dogged determination on both sides." That was Pershing looking back calmly on the situation long after the war. At the time that his opening drive was stopped on October 1, however, he was too furious to praise the determination of his tired troops. He ordered them to get moving forward again the next day "without regard of losses and without regard to the exposed conditions of the flanks. . . ."

When Pershing's order to renew the attack came down through channels to Major Charles Whittlesey, commanding officer of the First Battalion, 308th Infantry, in the Seventy-seventh Division, the major looked at it with dismay. He talked it over glumly with Captain George McMurtry, the acting commander of the 308th's Second Battalion, which was to advance in close support of Whittlesey's men the next morning.

Heavy casualties had already cut their battalions down to half strength; between them, they had only about eight hundred men instead of the regulation sixteen hundred. Moreover, their troops were exhausted. They had been moved into the Argonne sector from combat on the Aisne River with no rest and had experienced little sleep during the past month. The Seventy-seventh Division was a New York outfit, known as "The Times Square Division," with a Statue of Liberty emblem on its shoulder patches. But many of its original troops from Brooklyn, Manhattan, and the Bronx had recently been replaced by draftees from the Middle West who had had little or no basic training. A few days earlier one of them had been found calmly smoking behind some shrubbery during a battle. By way of explanation he gestured toward his rifle, saying, "I can't make the bullets go into this thing."

Along with his other worries, Whittlesey was particularly annoyed by the stipulation in Pershing's attack order that his battalion had to keep going forward even if its flanks were left exposed to the Germans. As Whittlesey's riflemen advanced along the extreme west side of the Argonne Forest, chronically laggard French troops moved through the open fields of the Aisne River Valley on their left flank. Only two days before, in the same area, German infiltrators had slipped around behind Whittlesey's left and had surrounded two of his companies for several hours. He was sure that it could happen again.

Whittlesey was not a field officer who could accept what seemed to him a dangerously illogical combat order without complaint. He was a stern and upright New England Yankee from Pittsfield, Massachusetts, a graduate of Williams College, a tall, slim man who wore glasses and looked rather like President Woodrow Wilson. He was also a precise Wall Street lawyer who had given up his practice to take the reserve officers' refresher course at Plattsburg when the war broke out. George McMurtry, his fellow battalion commander, was a Wall Street attorney, too, but their resemblance ended there. McMurtry, a husky and cheerful New Yorker who later made a million dollars in the stock market, had served with Theodore Roosevelt's Rough Riders in the Spanish-American War battle of San Juan Hill. But he agreed with Whittlesey that carrying out the order seemed impossible.

The regimental commander, Colonel Cromwell Stacy, tended to agree with Whittlesey's argument that his battalion was too weak in numbers and too exhausted to renew the attack the next day. The colonel also saw the danger of an outflanking movement by the Germans. He passed along Whittlesey's complaints to the brigade commander, Brigadier General Evan M. Johnson, who thought enough of them to ask his division commander, Major General Robert Alexander, if the attack could at least be postponed to give the troops a little more rest. Alexander was the type of ramrod general who had urged his Seventy-seventh Division before the start of the September 26 offensive to "Fight hard, keep your spirits high and your bayonets bright!" He sent word back to Stacy that the attack would start the next morning as scheduled.

When Stacy passed the order on to Whittlesey, the major saluted and said, "All right. I'll attack, but whether you'll hear from me again I don't know."

The morning of the attack, October 2, was foggy and wet. Field kitchens that were supposed to serve a hot breakfast to the 308th Battalion never appeared, and the shivering riflemen chewed hardtack and canned corned beef while they listened to the half-hour artillery barrage that was supposed to clear the route of their advance. At 6:30 rockets flashed in the gray sky, signaling the time to move forward along the twenty-mile Argonne front, and the infantrymen and machine gunners stood up and filed into the thick underbrush. Whittlesey himself led the way, close behind the forward scouts, his pistol in one hand and a pair of barbed-

wire cutters in the other. It was unusual for a battalion commander to be in front of advancing infantry troops, but Whittlesey wanted to make sure that his forward squads were heading in the right direction and keeping in contact with each other in the confusing tangle of trees and foliage.

The orders of the day called for Whittlesey and McMurtry to lead their battalions almost straight north, through a sector of the German line that ran across a long ravine with steep slopes on both sides. For starters, this seemed impossible. On the high ground above both sides of the ravine there were enemy machine gun and mortar shelling emplacements that could pour heavy fire on the slopes below. If they could get through the ravine, the two battalions were to keep moving north and up a slope to a point on high ground beyond Charlevaux Brook where an ancient Roman road ran eastward from Charlevaux Mill. There they were to dig in, establish liaison with the French troops on their left and another brigade of their own Seventy-seventh Division on the right, and await further orders.

Whittlesey advanced during the morning into the ravine, with three of his rifle companies and three of McMurtry's companies deployed on its right slope. Much to his unease, two other companies, one of his and one from McMurtry's battalion, had to be placed on the left slope of the ravine, far from their commanders. By 10 o'clock the whole force was pinned down and its advance stopped by heavy fire from La Palette, the German fortification on the high ground at the left side of the ravine.

The Americans noticed to their surprise, however, that they were not getting much fire from the enemy gun emplacement above the east side of the ravine, named on the maps Hill 198. After lunch, when division headquarters ordered its troops to resume the attack, Whittlesey decided to switch the direction of his advance, staying away from La Palette's heavy gunfire on his left and taking a chance on hitting Hill 198 on the right. There, to his gratification, his battalion broke through the German line with McMurtry's men close behind, taking two German officers and twenty-eight enlisted men as prisoners and killing and wounding many others. The Americans learned later that the fortifications on Hill 198 had been manned by older enemy soldiers, men in their late forties and early fifties, who had been without food for two days. Most of them had deserted their posts during the morning's bombardment.

Whittlesey had little trouble pushing on

to his objective, the high ground beyond Charlevaux Brook, where he was to dig in for the night. He sent runners back to regimental headquarters to announce his position and ask for reinforcements. His small force had lost another ninety men in the afternoon's fighting, and the two rifle companies on the opposite side of the ravine were missing. The news of Whittlesey's drive through the German line was greeted with happy excitement at the Seventy-seventh Division's headquarters; it was the one and only successful attack of the day along the Argonne front. The French on Whittlesey's left flank had been stopped cold and, on his right, the Seventy-seventh's 153rd Brigade and the Twenty-eighth Pennsylvanian Division had been unable to move.

While they waited for support, with darkness falling, Whittlesey and McMurtry arranged their riflemen and machine gunners to form a pocket of resistance in an oval about three hundred yards wide and sixty yards deep. Machine guns were placed on both flanks, and teams equipped with Chauchat guns, a light French version of the Browning Automatic Rifle, dug in around the perimeter of the position. Overcoats and blankets had been left behind when the offensive started, and food and cigarettes were scarce; the officers learned that two of the infantry companies had brought no rations with them. After the defense lines were arranged, ration details were sent out. They never returned, but water was discovered in a spring south of the position.

The Germans in the Argonne Forest had lines of telephone communication, but Whittlesey's unit did not. To get a message back to his regimental command post, Whittlesey used a relay team of runners, posted at intervals in the woods behind him. Assigning riflemen to duty as runners seriously depleted the fire power of his infantry companies, but the major considered human messengers more reliable than the carrier pigeons that were his only other means of communication. Omer Richards, a French Canadian private from upstate New York who was the caretaker of the First Battalion's pigeons, had carried a cage with eight birds during the advance through the enemy line. The pigeons were trained to fly back to a loft at division headquarters, each carrying a message written on a slip of rice paper in a metal capsule attached to one of its legs. Whittlesey's unit had also brought a heavy roll of white cotton sheeting, which was spread on the ground inside the perimeter of their defensive pocket to display the location of their position to any Allied plane that might fly over it.

When the news of Whittlesey's breakthrough reached the Seventy-seventh Division's headquarters, Major General Alexander immediately ordered a battalion of infantry from another regiment, then being held in reserve, to move forward that night as a reinforcement. Alexander was eagerly planning to capitalize on the opening in the German line by building up an offensive force in that narrow corridor strong enough to make an attack on the Giselher-Stellung, the main chain of enemy fortifications in the Argonne a few miles farther to the north. But only one of the four rifle companies sent into the pitch-dark woods to help Whittlesey managed to find him early the next morning—Captain Nelson Holderman's Company K from the 307th Infantry's Third Battalion. The arrival of this contingent of ninety-seven officers and enlisted men added little numerical strength to the band of survivors in the pocket. At about the time that Whittlesey and McMurtry welcomed Holderman, they sent Lieutenant Karl Wilhelm and fifty men from McMurtry's rifle companies off into the woods on the left in an attempt to find the two companies, D and F, that had been lost on that side of the ravine during the previous day's fighting. Wilhelm ran into a strong force of Germans who pinned his men down under heavy machine gun and grenade fire, killing or wounding most of them. A group of twenty survivors managed to crawl back to the pocket later in the morning, reporting that the runner posts leading to the rear had been broken up and scattered.

Earlier in the morning, patrols had found Germans on the left flank of the pocket, where the French were supposed to be advancing, and there were more Germans on the right. Whittlesey realized that his small pocket was being surrounded. He asked Holderman, a cheerful and willing Californian, to take his company and some scouts who knew the terrain back toward Hill 198 to clear out the enemy machine gun positions he suspected were being set up, and thus reestablish his line of runner posts to regimental headquarters.

Holderman found that Hill 198, almost deserted when Whittlesey had taken it the day before, had not only been reoccupied and heavily armed with machine guns by the Germans during the night, it was also surrounded by new barbed wire. When Holderman tried to advance on the hill, his men were hit by machine gun fire on their flanks and sniper fire from the woods behind them. Realizing that his company

was about to be cut off from the rear, Holderman turned around and fought his way back across Charlevaux Brook to the shelter of the pocket, with several wounded men staggering beside him.

When the German commanders had first heard, early the previous evening, that Whittlesey's small force had broken through their defense line, it never occurred to them that his detachment was an isolated group with no support behind it. They assumed that Whittlesey's men were an advance scouting party that would immediately be followed by a big American attacking force. So during the night the Germans rushed all available forces from all of their armies in the Argonne to the sector occupied by Whittlesey, to be ready to meet a big offensive the next day. When morning came, they had no trouble surrounding the circle of vastly outnumbered Americans and cutting off their line of communication.

By noon on October 3, Whittlesey, McMurtry, and Holderman realized that they were completely surrounded. A head count showed that after the casualties of the morning there were only 550 men left in the pocket, including some who had been severely wounded. McMurtry took a pad of message paper from his pocket, wrote on it, and showed the message to Whittlesey, who nodded. McMurtry called Corporal Walter Baldwin, the First Battalion message clerk, and told him to deliver the message to each of the company commanders. It read: "Our mission is to hold this position at all costs. No falling back. Have this understood by every man in your command."

Whittlesey sent a carrier pigeon to his division's headquarters with a message stating his exact position and his isolation, and asking for reinforcements and artillery support. The pigeon delivered the message, but Major General Alexander, who already knew that Whittlesey had been cut off, could do nothing for him. All of the division's reserve troops were in combat on the front line, some of them supporting the embattled French on Whittlesey's left and others with the hard-pressed Seventy-seventh Division's 153rd Brigade on his right. The general's big hopes of the night before for using Whittlesey's gap as the doorway for a smashing drive against the Giselher-Stellung line had dissolved during the discouraging morning.

That afternoon, after the men in the pocket had eaten their last scraps of food, the Germans blasted them with mortar fire and grenades and made the first of many attempts to send riflemen crawling

into the enclosure. The attackers were turned back by machine gun and automatic rifle fire, but at nightfall Whittlesey reported by carrier pigeon that one third of the men in his force had been killed or seriously wounded and all of his bandages and medical supplies had been used up. He asked for food and ammunition to be dropped from the air and again pleaded for artillery support.

During that night's darkness, any sound of movement or a groan of pain from a wounded man would draw a burst of machine gun fire from the Germans. The men in the pocket tried to be as quiet as possible while they struggled to dig burial holes for their dead. The burly George McMurtry crawled from one company to another, whispering the words of encouragement that he repeated over and over again that week, "Everything is practically okay." He pleaded with one soldier, who had been shot through his stomach, to be silent. "It pains like hell, Captain," the man said, "but I'll keep as quiet as I can." He died a half hour later without uttering another sound.

The next morning, Friday, October 4, one of Holderman's patrols reported a gap in the German line on the pocket's rear right flank. Whittlesey and McMurtry debated about retreating through that opening, but quickly decided against it when they realized that they would have to leave their wounded men behind. During the morning, Whittlesey used two of his remaining four carrier pigeons to remind the division headquarters that he needed medical supplies and food and to report that his D and F companies were still missing on the left side of the ravine behind him. He did not know that about one hundred men from the two companies still in action had made an attempt to reach him the previous day but had been beaten back under fire from La Palette and Hill 198.

Early that afternoon an Allied plane swooped low over the pocket, turned, and flew back to the rear. The officers felt encouraged; it was the first plane they had seen since they had been trapped. Now maybe supplies would be dropped to them. A few minutes later a barrage of artillery fire exploded behind the pocket to the southeast. "It's ours!" somebody yelled.

A few men stood up and cheered. Then the exploding bursts of fire moved slowly toward the pocket and into the middle of the American position, knocking down trees and throwing up showers of turf and foliage. The officers, assuming that the barrage would soon move on to the German lines, tried to quiet their panic-stricken men. Whittlesey left his command post hole to walk around in the open, trying to put on a show of calm. McMurtry shouted, "Take it easy! This won't last long!"

But the heavy downpour of American shellfire kept on smashing and roaring all over the pocket. Walter Baldwin, trying to lead a wounded friend to cover, was joined by Private Robert Manson, Whittlesey's orderly, and the First Battalion's sergeant major, Ben Gaedeke. A shell exploded on them, tearing out the wounded man's chest. Gaedeke's body disappeared completely. "We could only find his helmet and his pistol," Manson said later. Baldwin was picked up and hurled away, deafened and half unconscious.

There were only two pigeons left in Omer Richards' cage. Whittlesey wrote a message and handed it to Richards: "We are along the road parallel 276.4. Our own artillery is dropping a barrage directly on us. For heaven's sake, stop it."

While Richards was nervously taking one of the pigeons out of the cage, the bird fluttered out of his hands and flew away. That left only one pigeon, a favorite named Cher Ami, or Dear Friend. Richards clipped the message to Cher Ami's leg, cupped the bird in his hands, and tossed it up into the sky. The pigeon flew in a circle or two, them calmly came to rest on a branch of a nearby tree.

Whittlesey and Richards shouted at Cher Ami, clapped their hands, and waved their helmets. The bird eyed them and refused to move. They picked up stones and threw them at the pigeon. Richards shinnied up the trunk of the tree and shook the branch where the bird was sitting. At last, Cher Ami fluttered his wings and flew away through a storm of German rifle fire and a shower of shrapnel from the distant American guns.

The barrage thundered on for another two hours, until Cher Ami reached the pigeon loft and a telephone message from the division headquarters finally put a stop to it.

That was a night of agonized suffering and hunger in the pocket. Even many of the unwounded men were too weak to join in the work of digging graves. The next day, Saturday, October 5, Allied planes flew overhead and dropped food and ammunition, but the supplies landed beyond the German lines, which were only a few yards away. By now, the trapped Americans and the German troops surrounding them were shouting insults at each other. Sometimes when a German officer called the roll of the names in his company, the Americans would yell back in reply. At one point in the siege, a German yelled to the Yanks in a voice with an apparently British accent, "I say, you chaps! You haven't a chance! Why not surrender while there's still time?"

One American shouted back, "Who's that? The Prince of Wales?" And another added, "I thought the Limeys were on our side!"

Whittlesey's plight was now well known not only in Pershing's First Army Headquarters but all over the United States. A United Press correspondent, Fred S. Ferguson, had filed a dramatic report on the trapped force of Americans that was headlined at home as the story of "the Lost Battalion." Pershing was embarrassed by the widely publicized account of his army's failure to save the small band of brave survivors. He sent a stern order that Saturday morning to General Alexander at the Seventy-seventh Division that said, "I direct that a vigorous effort be made this afternoon to relieve the companies on the left of the Seventy-seventh Division that are cut off."

Whittlesey's regimental commander, the same Colonel Stacy who had relayed the major's complaints about the order to attack earlier in the week, was then leading a hard-pressed force in the ravine behind the pocket. Stacy flatly refused to lead an assault on the Germans between his position and Whittlesey's pocket unless he was reinforced by fresh troops.

When the brigade commander, General Johnson, passed on this message to General Alexander, the division commander blew up, and ordered Johnson to relieve Stacy and see that the assault went forward.

Johnson, a 57-year-old brigadier with thirty-six years in the Regular Army, gave Stacy's regimental command to a captain—he had no lieutenant colonels or majors left—and then personally led a company of eighty-five riflemen up the ravine toward Whittlesey's position. After ninety minutes of hard fighting, and receiving a leg wound from a machine gun bullet, the one-star general was forced to halt his advance and turn back, leaving twenty of his men dead or wounded behind him.

Whittlesey's dwindling survivors in the isolated pocket endured the most frightening ordeal of the week the next day, Sunday, October 6, when Germans carrying flame throwers advanced into their lines of defense. Some of the Americans backed off in terror from the jets of flame that flashed a hundred feet in front of the crouching attackers. Holderman, now severely wounded, with a grenade fragment imbedded in his back, and leaning on two rifles for support, directed a barrage

Captain George McMurtry in more tranquil times: aboard the S.S. America, *bound for home*

A FRIEND IN NEED

Somewhere in the endless collections of the Smithsonian Institution are the stuffed remains of Cher Ami, and in the case with them is a Croix de Guerre. The bird won the decoration in spite of himself, so to speak, for he was most reluctant to take off on his homing mission back to headquarters. Yet it is not an overstatement to say that Cher Ami saved the Lost Battalion. And when he finally wheeled out of the besieged pocket with Whittlesey's last, desperate message, Cher Ami—who was about to become the most famous pigeon in history—was taking part in a military tradition that went back forty years.

The army bought its first homing pigeons in 1878, and packed them out to the 5th Infantry Regiment, which was on duty in the Dakota Territory. But the 5th never learned how effective pigeons could be, for large numbers of hawks in the area put a speedy end to the experiment. A decade later, however, the army established a loft at Key West, and when Pershing led his punitive expedition into Mexico in 1916 there were pigeons in the van.

Shortly after America entered the First World War, the birds were made an official part of the Signal Corps, and the AEF went overseas with a pigeon communication unit of four officers, 324 men, and more than seven thousand birds.

The first pigeons got to France in November, 1917, and were immediately put into service. By the time the Meuse-Argonne offensive was launched, there were only four mobile lofts available. "Though not sufficiently trained for the highest type of service," says the Signal Corps with good military phlegm, "[the pigeons] acquitted themselves well." The birds took 27 per cent casualties in their ranks, but they got through with four hundred messages during the offensive. Cher Ami was with them. He delivered twelve messages while he was on the Verdun front, but his most important flight was his last.

After he left the pocket, carrying Whittlesey's plea to lift the American barrage that was destroying his command, Cher Ami was struck by a bullet that carried away one leg and shattered his breastbone. But he flapped on, and collapsed half an hour later on the roof of the loft at Rampont, twenty-five miles away. The vital message was still hanging from a torn leg tendon.

The division veterinarian dressed Cher Ami's wounds and reportedly whittled a wooden leg for him. The bird recuperated quickly, and was in good shape when the French gave him the Croix de Guerre with palm (Citation à l'ordre de l'Armée). General Pershing saw Cher Ami off when the bird sailed home in triumph on the transport *Ohioan* in the company of other heroic pigeons, among them President Wilson, who was wounded on the Verdun front, and Spike, who had delivered fifty-two messages.

But Cher Ami did not have long to enjoy the fruits of peace and the rewards of glory. He died at Fort Monmouth, New Jersey, on June 13, 1919. —R.F.S.

U.S. SIGNAL CORPS, NATIONAL ARCHIVES

of automatic rifle fire that dropped all of the flame operators, setting some ablaze in their own spilled fuel. But during the German assault, which went on for more than two hours, a few Americans and two of their machine guns were captured and several more of Whittlesey's men were killed and seriously wounded.

At dawn the next day, October 7, a group of nine famished enlisted men from one of McMurtry's companies crawled through the German lines searching for packages of food that had been dropped from American planes the day before. They were trapped by an enemy patrol. Five were killed and the other four were wounded and taken prisoner. A German lieutenant who had spent six years as a tungsten salesman in Seattle, Washington, before the war questioned the prisoners and suggested to his commanding officer that one of them, a private named Lowell R. Hollingshead, be sent back to the American position with a surrender proposal. That afternoon Hollingshead approached the pocket's outposts, carrying a white flag and a note addressed to "The Commanding Officer of the 2nd Batl.," which said, in part:

"The suffering of your wounded man can be heared over here in the German lines and we are appealing to your human sentiments. A withe Flag shown by one of your man will tell us that you agree with these conditions.

"Please treat Private Lowell R. Hollingshead as an honourable man. He is quite a soldier. We envy you."

Whittlesey and McMurtry read the note and showed it to Holderman. Walter Baldwin, who was there, recalled later that the three officers smiled at each other and McMurtry said, "They're begging us to quit. They're more worried than we are."

Whittlesey did not bother to send a reply but immediately ordered that the white sheeting spread on the ground as a marker for Allied aircraft be rolled up and put under cover. The major did not want it mistaken as a surrender signal by the Germans.

When word of the surrender offer spread through the pocket, it lifted the spirits of the exhausted survivors. The unusual quiet of the late afternoon was broken by one American who sat up and shouted, "You Heinie bastards, come and get us!" followed by a chorus of loud obscenities from his comrades. The Germans replied with a heavy attack that was beaten back as Holderman, leaning on his rifle crutches and firing his Colt .45, called orders to the one remaining machine gunner. The captain already had four wounds, including the grenade fragment

in his back, when the day's fighting began; he later recalled that he had received his fifth wound about the same time that he shot his fifth German.

As darkness fell that night, Whittlesey and McMurtry wondered how they could survive through another day. Ammunition had almost run out, and the men in the pocket were too weak and tired to dig any more graves.

Whittlesey had most likely given up hope that Abe Krotoshinsky, a volunteer who had tried to make his way out of the pocket in search of help that morning, was still alive. Two other men who had gone off with Krotoshinsky came back reporting that they had been spotted and pinned down by enemy machine gun fire. Both thought Krotoshinsky had been killed.

But shortly after 7 o'clock that evening Lieutenant Richard Tillman and a patrol of riflemen from the Seventy-seventh Division's nearby 307th Infantry walked into the pocket without firing a shot.

After Whittlesey's small force had been trapped, Pershing had rushed the experienced veterans of the First Infantry Division, "The Big Red One," into action in the Aire River valley on the east side of the forest. There they scored a major break-through in the German line of defense. That staggering blow weakened the enemy's hold on the Argonne sector and finally enabled the Americans behind Whittlesey and the French on his left to move forward. Now the Germans who had asked Whittlesey to surrender a few hours earlier found themselves in danger of being surrounded. Unknown to Whittlesey and McMurtry, their besiegers had silently pulled back and retreated to the north shortly after sundown.

Some reports say that Tillman's patrol was guided to the pocket by Abe Krotoshinsky, who was in fact awarded the Distinguished Service Cross for his bravery. Other survivors recalled that Tillman's men were already handing out cans of corned beef by the time Krotoshinsky returned with another patrol of Americans. Anyway, by then the Germans were gone and the five-day siege had ended with no surrender.

The next morning 190 of the 500 Americans who had been trapped in the pocket earlier in the week were able to walk back through the valley to their regimental headquarters. Another 190 were seriously wounded, 107 were dead, and 63 were missing. Shortly after daybreak, when the ambulances were arriving, Corporal Baldwin, the message clerk, saw an officer with two stars on his cap walking along the old Roman road toward the pocket, swinging

a malacca cane. It was Major General Alexander, the Seventy-seventh Division's commander.

"Where's Whittlesey?" he wanted to know.

"Down at the foot of the hill, sir," said Baldwin, pointing toward where the major was personally passing out food to his men. "Shall I get him for you?"

"By no means," said the general. "I'll go to him."

Whittlesey, McMurtry, and Holderman were awarded the Congressional Medal of Honor. In later years, the jovial McMurtry enjoyed attending the Lost Battalion's reunion dinners and picked up the check for most of them until he died in 1958 at the age of eighty-two. Whittlesey came home tense and uncomfortable as an acclaimed war hero, besieged by invitations to civic and charitable banquets that he found almost as strenuous as the Argonne siege. A bachelor, engrossed in his work as a lawyer on Wall Street, he wanted to forget the war. A friend remembered him complaining, "Not a day goes by but I hear from some of my old outfit, usually about some sorrow or misfortune. I cannot bear much more. I want to be left in peace."

On Armistice Day in 1921, Whittlesey, McMurtry, and other Medal of Honor winners attended the dedication of the new Tomb of the Unknown Soldier at Arlington National Cemetery. Whittlesey had little to say to anybody and seemed ill at ease. Two weeks later, on Thanksgiving Day, he boarded a ship that was sailing on a holiday cruise to Havana. That evening, when liquor was served outside the three-mile limit, he sat up late in the saloon drinking with another passenger. Then, announcing that he was going to bed, he went on deck and jumped overboard.

Joe McCarthy, a frequent contributor to our pages, is at work on two books: a narrative history of the World War II battle for Normandy and a memoir of twenty-five years as a magazine journalist.
OVERLEAF: *The walking wounded of the 308th Infantry slowly make their way out of the splintered Argonne Forest at the end of their ordeal, October 8, 1918.*
History of the 308th Infantry, 1917–1919, BY WARDLAW MILES, PUBLISHED BY G.P. PUTNAM'S SONS, NEW YORK, 1927

AMERICAN HERITAGE

Announces
The Presentation of the
1977
SAMUEL ELIOT MORISON AWARD
to
Joseph P. Lash
for
Roosevelt and Churchill, 1939–1941:
The Partnership That Saved the West

If Joseph P. Lash had decided, back in 1942, to write a book on the wartime friendship between Franklin D. Roosevelt and Winston Churchill, he would have been off to a lucky start. He happened to be a guest at the White House on the occasion of the British leader's first transatlantic visit after Pearl Harbor, and found himself seated next to the famous man at lunch.

"I was too awe-struck to open my mouth," Lash reported later. "There was no necessity. The language cascaded out of him. In my journal I wrote: 'He is an exuberant, enormously strong personality, exciting, full of temperament, witty, his phrases resonant with the vigors of the best English stylists, his talk full of imagery.'"

These were appropriate observations for a young writer who, thirty-five years later, would win AMERICAN HERITAGE's first award of the Samuel Eliot Morison prize for "the best book on American history by an American author that sustains the tradition that good history is literature as well as high scholarship." And the subject of that book, published in 1976 by W. W. Norton & Company, is indeed the wartime friendship between Roosevelt and Churchill.

Actually, back there in the days just after Pearl Harbor, Joe Lash hardly thought of himself as a writer; he was more (as he puts it) "a political person." A native New Yorker, he was active in the newly formed American Student Union in the thirties until, in 1939, he met Eleanor Roosevelt—and fell under her spell. It was the start of a close friendship that moved him from the far

Prizewinner Joseph P. Lash in New York
PHOTOGRAPH © 1977 BY JILL KREMENTZ

left into the vanguard of liberal Democratic politics and lasted until Mrs. Roosevelt's death in 1962.

Lash never saw Winston Churchill again after that brief meeting in 1942, since he entered the Army shortly thereafter and served—mostly as a weather observer and forecaster for the Air Force in the Solomon Islands—until the end of the war. A correspondent and editorial writer for the New York *Post* from 1950 to 1966, he covered the United Nations for many years and, besides furthering his friendship with Mrs. Roosevelt, became well acquainted with the UN Secretary-General. This prompted his first biography, *Dag Hammarskjöld: Custodian of the Brushfire Peace* (1961). A short memoir of Mrs. Roosevelt that Lash wrote soon after she died led to his being chosen to do her authorized

biography, based on three years of work among the First Lady's papers at Hyde Park. The result was the extraordinary *Eleanor and Franklin* (1971), which won the National Book Award for biography in 1972, the Pulitzer Prize for that year in the same category, and the Francis Parkman Prize given by the Society of American Historians. It also was a Book-of-the-Month Club selection, as was its sequel, *Eleanor; The Years Alone*, which appeared in 1972.

Roosevelt and Churchill, as its subtitle suggests, is an account, meticulously documented, of the tremendous cooperative effort by which F.D.R. and the prime minister tried to prepare America to come into the struggle against Hitler. Pearl Harbor clinched the matter, and from then on Great Britain and the United States were, as

Mr. Lash puts it in his final chapter, "all in the same boat."

Mr. Lash and his wife Trude have an apartment in New York City, a home in Oakland, New Jersey, and a summer place on Martha's Vineyard, where the author does much of his writing. He is presently at work on a sequel that will trace the relationship between Roosevelt, Churchill, and Stalin through the end of World War II in Europe.

AMERICAN HERITAGE is proud to make its first award of the annual Morison prize of $5,000 to Mr. Lash.

SELLING THE SWEDISH NIGHTINGALE

Jenny Lind and P. T. Barnum

by Ruth Hume

When it comes to the performing arts, Americans have often suffered from a sense of cultural inferiority. Foreign artists are considered somehow better—more glamorous, more gifted, more refined—than our own. We have lavished our applause on the likes of Bernhardt, Burton, and Garbo, reserved our stormiest bravos for Paderewski, Chaliapin, and Nureyev, and lost our national composure over Lola Montez, Anna Held, and the Beatles. In the nineteenth century, American opera companies drew best when billed as Italian; even today American performers frequently find it pays to conquer Europe before wowing them in Omaha. The late Sol Hurok was the most successful modern impresario to profit from this fascination with foreign stars. But his triumphs paled—as did those of all his predecessors and their exotic imports—when compared to what happened in 1850 when P. T. Barnum brought the Swedish singer Jenny Lind to America.

High culture was not the forty-year-old master showman's usual métier. Believing that the American people loved to be humbugged, he built his reputation by ballyhooing such frauds as a "Feejee Mermaid" (fashioned from the body of a fish and the head and paws of a monkey) and a wrinkled old black woman whom he billed as "George Washington's one-hundred-and-sixty-one-year-old nurse." But he had nothing against the real goods—provided they could be made to turn a profit.

In 1850 Jenny Lind was probably the most famous performer in Europe. She had everything: a thrilling voice, dramatic talent, and a reputation for piety, modesty, and good works. Her success had been dazzling. When she appeared on the streets of Germany and Austria, male admirers rushed to unhitch the horses from her carriage and pull it themselves. It was said that when she sang in London the House of Commons could not obtain a quorum, and the royal court once postponed its annual visit to Scotland. Even Queen Victoria had thrown a bouquet at her feet in tribute.

To composers like Chopin, Berlioz, Meyerbeer, Schumann, and Mendelssohn her musicianship was a revelation. "There will not be born in a whole century another being so gifted as she," announced Mendelssohn, and he tailored the soprano part of "Elijah" expressly to her voice. Hans Christian Andersen heard her sing in Copenhagen in 1834 and lost his heart to her; he wrote that he had "seen a vestal virgin," and he courted her in vain for years with stories she inspired (Jenny coldhearted in "The Snow Queen"; Jenny warmhearted in "The Emperor's Nightingale").

Born in Stockholm in 1820, Jenny was the illegitimate daughter of an ill-natured schoolteacher named Anne-Marie Felborg and a good-natured wastrel named Nikla Lind. At the age of nine she was discovered in storybook fashion. She was sitting at her window one day, serenading her cat, when a ballerina's maid passed by, heard her extraordinary voice, and rushed off to tell her mistress about it. The dancer arranged an audition for Jenny, and she was accepted as a student at the Royal Theater School. By the time she was seventeen, she was one of the most valuable musical properties in Sweden; at twenty she was a member of the Swedish Royal Academy and court singer to the king.

In 1841 her voice seemed to have worn out, and she left Stockholm for Paris to try to save it. She had learned much about acting, dancing, and repertory at the Royal Theater School, but proper breathing and a secure vocal technique had not been part of her training, and too many demanding roles had taken a heavy toll. In Paris, she studied with Manuel Garcia, a renowned vocal teacher who showed her how to sing all over again. When she returned to the stage—more often in Austria and Germany than in Stockholm, to the chagrin of her Swedish admirers—she was a sensation. She then traveled to London in 1847 where, amid new triumphs, she was called "the Swedish Nightingale."

Jenny Lind and Victorian England were made for each other. In an era when

The product and the peddler: Jenny Lind (at left) as her public liked to think she was—beautiful, pious, and exquisitely refined. Above, Phineas Taylor Barnum, who knew a winning combination when he saw one.

LEFT: BROWN BROTHERS. ABOVE: CULVER

many opera stars were notorious courtesans, the emergence of a militantly virtuous singer (the "prima donna immaculata," the German poet Heine cynically called her) was a novelty. Other prima donnas may have reigned as queens of the demimonde, but no singer had previously been a houseguest of the Bishop of Norwich. In fact, the bishop's invitation had required some courage. For a stage performer to be received at court was one thing, at an Episcopal palace quite another. Nor was it universally condoned. "It is very right and proper," wrote one appalled clergyman, "that jackdaws should build in the church. They have vested interests there. But farewell the primitive purity of the establishment which affords a resting-place for nightingales." Nonetheless, this was a minority view. Jenny's demure virtue opened doors for herself and made it easier for performers who came after her to become respectable.

Her unusual acceptance in high places made her, in turn, a seemly fiancée in the eyes of a Captain Claudius Harris. Jenny must have been smitten by the sight of him in a full-dress uniform; certainly he had nothing else to recommend him. She rushed into an engagement to him but kept pushing back the wedding date while she argued with him over details of the marriage contract. The brainless Captain Claudius was blessed with a protective mother who guided his hand during the negotiations. Jenny resisted a demand that she retire from the stage and sing only in church or for charity, and she also balked at a clause calling for her to turn over all of her considerable wealth to her future husband. But it was Claudius himself who doomed the marriage, falling asleep one night while Jenny was singing to him. Angry and hurt, she fled to the Continent in late 1849, hoping to forget Captain Claudius and his mum.

It was then that P. T. Barnum came into her life. Though he had never seen or heard Jenny Lind, the American showman had read about her triumphs while touring Europe with his first great attraction, General Tom Thumb, in 1845 and 1846. He knew that concert halls sold out wherever she appeared; that she was celebrated for her virtue; and that she had delighted the crowned heads of Europe (an achievement always appealing to otherwise democratic Americans). He decided to bring her to the United States.

Barnum dispatched a smooth-talking Englishman named John Wilton to track

Jenny Lind's tumultuous arrival in New York on September 1, 1850
BROWN BROTHERS

her down and make her an offer. He was prepared to go as high as $1,000 a night for up to 150 concerts, plus expenses, but he hoped to achieve his goal for far less. As an incentive to sharp bargaining, he offered Wilton a sliding-scale commission based on his success in softening Jenny's terms: the better the deal Wilton made, the higher the commission he would receive. But when Jenny finally agreed to see Wilton in Lübeck, she opened the interview by announcing that she already had four offers to tour America and one to tour Russia. What exactly did Mr. Barnum have in mind? Wilton realized that this was no time for haggling, and he presented Barnum's top offer.

After checking Barnum's credit rating with his London bank, Jenny accepted. But she also insisted on the services of Julius Benedict, a German conductor, composer, and pianist with whom she had worked in England, and of Italian baritone Giovanni Belletti as assisting artist. (Solo recitals were still unknown in America.) Benedict's fee was $25,000; Belletti's half that. In addition, Barnum was to pay for a secretary, a maid, and a manservant, plus the cost of a sixty-piece orchestra and a carriage and pair in each city the tour played.

When Wilton reached New York in February, Barnum took all this in stride. But, he learned, there was still one more stipulation. The total fee for all three artists—$187,500—had to be deposited in advance with the banking house of Baring Brothers in London before Jenny would budge from Europe. Barnum had not bargained for this; he was accustomed to a more casual, pay-as-you-go system. But he remained optimistic, even when New York bankers refused to accept a percentage of the Lind tour as collateral for a loan to be sent to London. Undaunted, Barnum mortgaged everything he owned, and when he still came up short, persuaded a Philadelphia minister who thought Jenny would be a good influence on American morals to lend him the final $5,000.

Yet even Barnum must have had moments of doubt. Few Americans had ever heard of Jenny Lind. An encounter with a conductor on a railroad train from Philadelphia to New York drove the point home. Barnum proudly told the trainman that he had just signed a contract with Jenny Lind and she would be coming to America for an extended tour.

"Jenny Lind!" replied the conductor. "Is she a dancer?"

Barnum clearly had his work cut out for him. If this was all Americans knew

Myth and reality: the previously unpublished portrait by Louis Lang (above left) and the sentimental lithograph (left) reflect the public's ethereal image of the young singer. The daguerreotypes above reveal that the real Jenny was made of sturdier stuff.

BIRD SONG.

Creating a star: decorative prints like the one directly above familiarized the public with Jenny Lind—along with her supporting cast, baritone Giovanni Belletti and conductor Julius Benedict. Specially printed song sheets (above right) linked Jenny's repertoire with her name. Barnum's shrewd publicity resulted in an overwhelming demand for tickets (right) to Jenny Lind concerts everywhere she played.

TOP LEFT: HARVARD THEATRE COLLECTION. TOP RIGHT: BOTH BMI ARCHIVES. RIGHT: BOTH HARVARD THEATRE COLLECTION

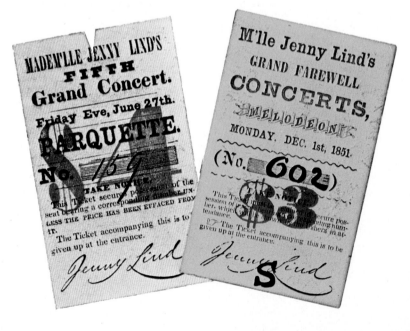

of "the greatest songstress in the world," he wrote, "I am not sure that six months will be too long a time for me to occupy in enlightening the public in regard to her merits."

The "enlightening" began right away. Barnum's first announcement to the press set the tone. "A visit from such a woman," he proclaimed, "who regards her high artistic powers as a gift from Heaven, for the amelioration of affliction and distress . . . . will be a blessing to America." Next came an authorized biographical pamphlet and photograph. "It is her intrinsic worth of heart and delicacy of mind," the pamphlet said, that produced Jenny's vocal "potency." Barnum correctly surmised that Jenny's piety and her history of giving frequent benefit concerts for hospitals and orphanages would weigh more with the nonmusical public than the fact that the singer had a range of two and a half octaves and an extraordinary trill.

As Jenny's arrival in America grew nearer, Barnum doubled and redoubled his efforts to drum up interest. Jenny had turned down engagements in Europe during her last weeks there in order to rest up for the voyage. But at Barnum's urgent request she agreed to give a pair of concerts in Liverpool, her port of embarkation. As he expected, the fact that the two Liverpool concerts were Jenny's last ones before sailing for the wilds of America brought an unprecedented surge of affection from her British public. There was a frenzied demand for tickets to the farewell events. The first took place on August 16, the night before the regular Saturday transatlantic ship cast off for America. Barnum had ordered his British agent to go to London and, as he delicately put it, "Procure the services of a musical critic." The critic was hastened to Liverpool to cover the concert. He finished his review at 1:30 A.M. Barnum's man hotfooted it to the newspaper office, presumably paced nervously while the article went to press, then rushed copies of the early edition down to the dock. The review, detailing the unbridled enthusiasm of the Liverpool audience and its grief at Jenny's imminent departure, appeared in U.S. newspapers a week before her arrival.

Barnum's bag of tricks was bottomless. Next, he wrote a letter addressed to himself and signed it with the name of composer Julius Benedict, who was traveling with Jenny. It appeared in the New York *Daily Tribune* on August 14. "I have just heard Mlle. Jenny Lind," the "Benedict" letter announced, "whose

voice has acquired—*if that were possible*—even additional powers and effect by a timely and well-chosen repose. You may depend on it, that such a performance as hers—in the finest pieces of her *repertoire*—must warrant an unprecedented excitement. . . . Mlle. Lind is very anxious to give a Welcome to America in a kind of national song, which, if I can obtain the poetry of one of your first-rate literary men, I shall set to music, and which she will sing in addition to the pieces originally fixed upon."

The letter was followed with Barnum's own announcement that the "Nightingale's" request for a "national song" would be filled by means of a public contest. He offered $100—soon raised to $200—for a winning poem, entries to be received by "P. T. Barnum, Esq., New York." Seven hundred and fifty-three hastily written efforts were received. The winner was the poet and world traveler Bayard Taylor. He needed $200 as much as the next poet, but he later admitted that the Jenny Lind Prize Song was always a source of embarrassment to him. It began:

> *I greet with a full heart the*
> *Land of the West*
> *Whose Banner of Stars o'er a*
> *world is unrolled;*
> *Whose empire o'ershadows*
> *Atlantic's wide breast,*
> *And opes to the sunset its*
> *gateway of gold!*
> *The land of the mountain, the*
> *land of the lake,*
> *And rivers that roll in*
> *magnificent tide—*
> *Where the souls of the mighty*
> *from slumber awake,*
> *And hallow the soil for whose*
> *freedom they died!*

Prize poem in hand, Barnum had yet to break the news of it to Jenny and Benedict, still in mid-ocean blissfully unaware of the whole business. No evidence of his legendary powers of persuasion is more impressive than the fact that he later got Benedict to set Taylor's dreadful lines to music and talked Jenny into singing them.

As the S.S. *Atlantic* entered New York harbor, Barnum and a reporter for the New York *Tribune* rode out aboard the quarantine boat that went to meet it. Barnum carried a bouquet of red roses, which presented certain problems when it came time to clamber up the rope ladder that hung from the side of the large vessel. Barnum opened a few buttons and manfully shoved the prickly bouquet into his vest, then hauled his considerable

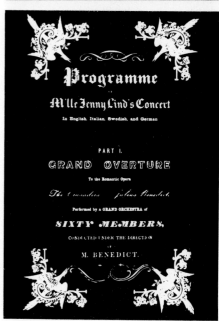

The Grand Opening: Jenny's immediate success with American audiences is depicted above in a detail from a Nathaniel Currier lithograph celebrating her first appearance at Castle Garden on September 11, 1850. The "programme" for the glamorous event was elaborate.

bulk aboard. When the ship's captain ushered him into the presence of his star, he was annoyed to find her already holding a bouquet three times the size of his own. The owner of the shipping line had beaten him to it by boarding the vessel at Sandy Hook.

The *Tribune* correspondent's report was more realistic than most. "Jenny," he noted, was "rather more robust in face and person than her portraits would indicate." Her mouth and nose "though molded on the large Swedish type convey an impression of benevolence and sound goodness of heart." (The reporter's surprise at her actual appearance was understandable: all the pictures of her that anyone in America had seen had come from England and were of the ethereal, disembodied-spirit type dearly loved by Victorian artists.)

Perhaps forty thousand persons greeted Jenny's ship when it finally docked on Sunday, September 1, 1850. She and her entourage made their way through the adoring crowds to Barnum's carriage. The showman himself leaped into the driver's seat "as a legitimate advertisement," he explained later. "My presence on the outside of the carriage aided those who filled windows and sidewalks along the whole route in coming to the conclusion that Jenny Lind had arrived!"

She had indeed. Enthusiastic throngs milled around the Irving House Hotel all night, cheering and calling her name. They cheered even louder when two hundred members of the Musical Fund Society, escorted by a company of firemen in red flannel shirts, joined the crowd and began a nightlong serenade.

Barnum was gratified by the turnout. He had not been entirely sure what size concert hall Jenny needed. Now he knew. He hired the largest in town, Castle Garden, in Battery Park. Hundreds followed Jenny's carriage to and from rehearsals. New York merchants eagerly abetted Barnum's grand design by rushing into print to advertise hastily renamed Jenny Lind products: everything from Jenny Lind cigars to Jenny Lind sewing stands, gloves, scarves, riding hats, perfume (unfortunately for Jenny, the idea of paid endorsements was still far in the future).

Then, with the concert just five days away, Barnum staged another event that raised an even greater journalistic furor than the Prize Song Competition—the Great Jenny Lind Opening Concert Ticket Auction.

It had required discreet stage

managing. A few days before the auction, Barnum visited the office of his friend John N. Genin, a hatmaker, and offered him a golden opportunity: he would be the first man in America to buy a ticket to hear Jenny Lind sing. "Pay whatever you have to pay for the ticket," Barnum told him, "and consider it an investment in the future." Delighted, Genin agreed.

Barnum next visited a Dr. Brandreth, who made and widely advertised various patent medicines. "Buy the first Jenny Lind ticket at auction," Barnum recalled himself saying, "and let every newspaper in America, in Europe, announce that Dr. Brandreth, Jr., the maker of the celebrated Brandreth pills, secured the first Jenny Lind ticket at $50 or $100 as the case may be."

On the day of the great auction over three thousand people paid the admission fee of twelve and a half cents to enter Castle Garden. Among them were Genin's bookkeeper and Brandreth's cashier, each man's secret instructions unsuspected by the other. Brandreth's man opened at $25. Genin's came back with $50. Other bidders dropped away at $225; so did Brandreth's cashier. John N. Genin was the winner. And Barnum's prediction that possession of the first ticket would make his fortune proved true. So widely had reports of the auction been circulated that visitors to New York thereafter regarded Genin's shop as one of the town's major tourist attractions and bought Genin hats as souvenirs for the folks back home.

(The auction would be repeated in several cities where Jenny appeared. In Boston the first ticket went for $625. It was craftily purchased by a singer named Ossian F. Dodge, whose concert career from that moment on took a turn for the better. The highest-priced auction ticket was sold for $650 to Colonel William Ross of Providence, Rhode Island. Having outflanked his rivals around the country, the colonel failed to attend the concert. He did not like music.)

Jenny Lind's opening concert at Castle Garden—on September 11, 1850—was a landmark in the annals of the performing arts in America. Not even her frenetic advance publicity could make her performance an anticlimax. Seven thousand strong, the audience succumbed.

"Jenny Lind's first concert is over," the *Tribune*'s music critic wrote that night, "and all doubts are at an end. She is the greatest singer we have ever heard and her success is all that was anticipated from her genius and her fame."

Barnum later struck a commemorative medal of that wildly acclaimed event

5¢

1945.263

JENNY LIND

TRADE MARK PATENTED

MANUFACTURERS

NEW YORK-TAMPA CIGAR CO.

Lindomania: as Jenny's fame soared, so did the number of manufacturers who contrived ways to profit from America's obsession with her. Opposite page: a Jenny Lind bell and a pin box. This page: a paper doll set (top left and center); a candelabrum (top right); a needlecase cover (above left); an elegant fan (left); and—for the gentlemen—Jenny Lind cigars (above).

"The Lord loveth a cheerful giver," and hatter John Genin was so cheered by the increase in his business after he gave $225 for the first Jenny Lind concert ticket sold in America that he had this handsome poster made showing Jenny framed by a border of leaves, each recording a donation she had made to an American charity.
NEW-YORK HISTORICAL SOCIETY

and grandly presented one to each businessman or banker who had turned him down in his quest for $187,500.

Over the next two months Jenny performed concerts in Philadelphia, Boston, and in Providence, Rhode Island—where Brown University officials were forced to give infatuated students a half-holiday and suspended the rule that forbade any form of entertainment on week nights.

The legendary tour began in earnest in November—a seven-month royal progress that would take the entourage to fifteen U.S. cities, with a side excursion to Havana. The outpouring of love that greeted Jenny as she moved from town to town seemed ominous to the London *Times*. If a mere singer could, with the help of a "private adventurer," so arouse national enthusiasm, could not a political adventurer copy the method? "... the same reckless system of exaggeration, the same intense vulgarity of means ..." could be applied to fields other than music, the *Times* warned.

But this stern message from across the waters failed to dampen the Nightingale's reception in Washington. President Millard Fillmore himself called on Jenny at the Willard Hotel. The cabinet went to her concerts en masse. She even managed to cope with the fierce devotion of Daniel Webster, who attended several times, frequently rising and bowing to Jenny, and singing along whenever he knew the melody.

The Washington triumphs added a new item to Jenny's repertoire. Barnum had found a copy of a dimly remembered song called "Home, Sweet Home" from Sir Henry Bishop's otherwise forgettable opera *Clari*. The lyrics had been written by Boston poet John Howard Payne. Barnum had learned that Payne would attend the first concert. He urged Jenny to learn the song and to end the program with it, correctly surmising that after a plaintive rendition, sung by a presumably homesick Swedish girl to an aging American poet, there would not be a dry handkerchief in the house. The song created a furor, and it became a staple of Jenny's programs. Hastily reprinted by its publisher, it was soon firmly fixed on the national piano rack as one of America's favorite songs.

Barnum's contract with Jenny had called for 150 concerts at $1,000 each. After her Castle Garden triumph he had rewritten the agreement to give Jenny a percentage of the profits in addition to the fee. (Whether the idea for this renegotiation originated with Barnum, as he claimed, or with Jenny remains unclear.) But in the end she sang for him only ninety-five times. He had inserted a generous release clause into the contract, and on June 9, 1851, she notified him that she had had enough.

What happened to upset the markedly cordial relations between the two? Had Jenny, as one of the showman's ill-wishers maintained, revolted because Barnum had persuaded her to review a parade of elephants opening "Barnum's Great Asiatic Caravan, Museum and Menagerie"? Possibly. Had she been mortally offended at being booked into a hall that had recently housed animal acts? Who knows?

Barnum's own diagnosis of the problem makes as much sense as any other. Like most musical luminaries—before, since, and for all time—Jenny was surrounded by a gaggle of sycophants, a horde of "advisers" who, from the day of her arrival in America, had filled her ears with venomous anti-Barnum sentiments. He was cheapening her image, they told her. She would fare much better if she managed her own American career—with their help, naturally.

Barnum did not argue with her decision, and they parted friends. He was secretly delighted to see the end of the whole business. He had earned more than anyone had thought possible. The venture that was supposed to ruin him had brought in a total of $712,161.34— nearly three and a quarter million dollars in today's terms. In retrospect he would write of the tour that it "was an undertaking . . . bold in its conception, complete in its development, and astounding in its success. It was an enterprise never before or since equalled in managerial annals." Having achieved this pinnacle of entrepreneurial expertise, he was ready to return, at least temporarily, to the more peaceful atmosphere of his American Museum on Broadway.

Thus Jenny entered the concert management business on her own. Difficulties of which she had never dreamed arose in nearly every town— travel arrangements, hall rentals, ticket sales, things that had always seemed so simple, developed complications; pre-concert publicity dropped off alarmingly; so did audiences; the press became cooler, sometimes even hostile.

Jenny realized too late how much drudgery had been quietly absorbed by Barnum. By interposing himself between her and the public, he had always managed to keep what one writer called her "angel face" before the world. Now newspapers were beginning to comment on occasional "stingy" and "thundercloud" expressions. Toward the tour's end, another factor intervened that further cooled down America's love affair with Jenny Lind. His name was Otto Goldschmidt.

Otto was a serious young German musician—nearly ten years younger than Jenny—who had been a student of Mendelssohn. When Julius Benedict, exhausted by the pace, left the entourage and returned to London, Jenny sent for Otto to serve as her accompanist. Shortly thereafter she married him, and Otto proved to be a model husband.

Jenny's complete satisfaction with her spouse was not universally shared by her public. The image of her as a matron was somehow jarring, and many listeners recalled what one commentator had said: "Maidenhood is in her voice!" "Why is Madame Goldschmidt so much less than Jenny Lind?" *Harper's Monthly* asked itself. Because, it replied, "she who has conquered the world by song and goodness, has herself been conquered," and by one "no better, no worthier, no stronger than the average of men." Jenny did not help her cause by billing herself as "Madame Otto Goldschmidt (late Jenny Lind)."

Then there was the thorny question of Otto's solo work. Failing box-office receipts had caused Jenny to dismiss her orchestra and sing with piano alone. But the public had paid its money to hear Jenny sing, not to listen to Otto's long German piano works. The problem of spirited audience participation during Otto's offerings became so great that loyal Jenny took to seating herself conspicuously on the side of the stage and staring the audience down while her devoted consort played.

At last, Jenny decided wisely to end the tour and return to Europe. Her farewell American concert was sung at Castle Garden on May 24, 1852. This time the house was half empty. Barnum was out front and later went backstage to say good-by. He was too sportsmanlike to gloat. But as the Swedish Nightingale and her Otto finally sailed away, he must have thought of what a gala, historic, unforgettable farewell concert *he* could have staged for her.

The happy couple: Mr. and Mrs. Otto Goldschmidt sailed for England on May 29, 1852. They settled there and raised three children. Jenny never again sang operatic roles, having decided that God meant that she should devote her talents to religious music—which she did until her death in 1887.
BROWN BROTHERS

Ruth Hume has written several articles on music and American culture for AMERICAN HERITAGE.

For further reading: Humbug: the Art of P. T. Barnum, *by Neil Harris (Little, Brown and Company, 1973), and* Jenny Lind, the Swedish Nightingale, *by Gladys Shultz (J. B. Lippincott Company, 1962).*

The complicated problems of world peace, social justice, and international economics were all child's play to one S. Butchart, a turn-of-the-century Canadian of Owen Sound, Ontario. He had them all figured out, and had devised gloriously symbolic charts and diagrams with which to instruct the world. To assist the U.S. he sent this and seven similar self-portraits to President William McKinley in 1898. Alas, the President did not see them. An unimaginative clerk took one look and filed them away as the work of a crank. Who knows? Had McKinley figured them out, all that unpleasantness with Spain over Cuba might have been avoided.

This picture was found in the National Archives at Washington and was sent to us by Michael P. Musick of Greenbelt, Maryland.

* * * * *

We continue to invite our readers to send us unusual, dramatic, or "what's going on here?" photographs—at least thirty years old—that they own. They should be sent to Geoffrey C. Ward, American Heritage Publishing Co., 10 Rockefeller Plaza, N.Y., N.Y. 10020.

As we cannot be responsible for original material, we request that a copy be sent at first. Under no circumstances should glass negatives be mailed. Pictures can be returned only if accompanied by a stamped, self-addressed envelope. AMERICAN HERITAGE will pay $50.00 for each one that is run.

Let Me Make One Thing Perfectly Clear

CROSSWORDS IN HISTORY

Big Business

ACROSS

1 Very, in Vichy
5 Howard Thurston's source of income
10 Medics
14 Prosperity period
18 Dispossess
19 Rocket stage
20 Railroad owned by Gould and Fisk in 1867
21 Telephone conductor
22 Banker, philanthropist, art patron: 1867-1943
24 Transportation magnate: 1794-1877
26 Owners of businesses
27 Prefix with fascist or liberal
29 Seven-card melds in a card game
30 To—(exactly)
31 Muslim queen
33 Price-fixing, for instance: Slang
34 The consumer, to an adman
37 One who bequeaths money, etc.
39 Flinches; recoils
43 Shade of green
44 N. California county
45 Bien—, air base near Saigon
47 Chestnut-shipping town in N. Italy
48 U.S. aerial bombs
49 Ship that made wealth for Wouk
50 Sarnoff, the TV tycoon
52 GPO category
53 Dovekie
54 Mother in Madrid
55 Austere
56 Capital of Western Samoa
57 Craved
59 Steel magnate; Hoover's Secy. of Commerce: 1867-1948
61 Celebration, as for St. Rocco
62 "The wages of— death": Romans, VI, 23
63 Moon or Spoon
64 Industrialist who invented smokeless powder
67 Cigars for big spenders
69 *Winnie—Pu*
70 Mildness; mercy
71 Judge's mallet
72 Rich pharaoh, for short
74 Lon—, Cambodian leader
75 Department store moneymakers
76 Enthusiasm, as in a gold rush
77 Sundial number
78 Layers of irises
81 "Diamond—"
82 Conrad Hilton

83 Wagnerian tenor: 1870-1953
84 Avocado tree
86 Landlords are their payees
88 Head of the Playboy empire
89 French cherub
91 Warbucks of comics
92 King Cotton's bundle
93 Arab's source of wealth
97 Palm fiber
98 Money set apart by bankers
102 Physician who made a fortune in rubber: 1841-88
104 Baltimore iron merchant; great philanthropist: 1808-96
106 Butcher's son who made millions in fur trade: 1763-1848
107 Pelvic bones
108 Great lyric poet: 1875-1926
109 —Ferber, author of *Giant*
110 Author of *The Lemon Eaters:* 1968
111 Pearl Buck heroine
112 Weaver's reeds
113 Like Bergdorf Goodman's wares

investment
83 Wagnerian tenor: 1870-1953

DOWN

1 Premier behind the Pearl Harbor attack
2 Famed basketball coach at Kentucky
3 Salinger tale girl
4 Granaries, e.g.
5 Lodestone
6 June birthstone
7 Roman family group
8 Hypodermic: Abbr.
9 He said: "The man who dies rich dies disgraced"
10 Pious
11 —*pro nobis*
12 One of Carter's titles: Abbr.
13 R.E. Olds product
14 Family of a famed financial statistician
15 Final notice
16 Stewpot
17 Team owned by the Paysons
21 Skulls
23 They rise with inflation
25 "Paradise—"
28 First elected Governor of Alaska
31 *Games People Play* was his moneymaker
32 Colorado River group
34 Fictional plantation
35 Audibly
36 Standard Oil titan: 1839-1937

37 Founder of the periodical *Industrial Psychology*
38 Dick, Tom, or Sam
40 Kaiser-Frazer, e.g.
41 Puckish
42 VIP at Cairo
44 Transacted business
46 Source of wealth for Howard Hughes
49 Syndicates, combines, or trusts
50 Figure in red
51 Aid in childbirth
54 Egypt, to an Arab
55 Al Jolson's "boy"
56 Pulpit sign-off
58 Withered
59 Results of 1880's capital-labor disputes
60 Legal endorsement
62 Gave a commercial
64 Barracks decoration
65 "The Man—"
66 Like bulbs in a blackout
67 The rich
68 Accommodations for a top exec
71 Reputedly the world's wealthiest man (deceased)
73 Section of the Met
76 Loving couple
77 Surmised
79 "No creature so little—": Pope

80 Kind of partner
82 Andrew Mellon— hand in settling Europe's W.W.I debts
83 Stinging ant
85 Abraham Neiman in 1970
87 One of the Straus brothers
88 Jumbles
90 The river, in Oaxaca
92 *Vanity Fair* girl
93 Nigerian VIP's
94 Should that be the case
95 End-to-end extent: Abbr.
96 Item in Henry John Heinz's business
98 Part
99 —mecum (handbook)
100 Alcoholic heater
101 Symbol on an Armour product
103 D.C. hush-hush agcy.
105 Naught

Solution in the next issue

by Eugene T. Maleska

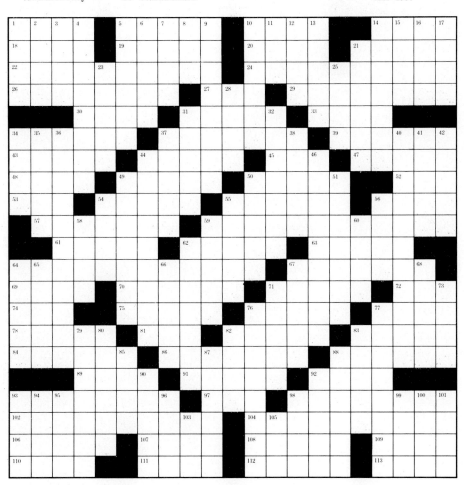

ON THE WHOLE, HE'D RATHER NOT BE IN PHILADELPHIA

This hitherto unpublished daguerreo-type was found in the same cache of photographs that included the slave portraits we published in our June, 1977, issue. All the pictures were apparently collected by Harvard scientist Louis Agassiz in the mid-nineteenth century to bolster his theory of "special creations" (which held that each race was a distinct species), and later came to be stored in the attic of Harvard's Peabody Museum.

This portrait was made by Frederick and William Langenheim, Philadelphia's most prestigious cameramen of the 1840's, but the brooding sitter was unidentified. Nonetheless, he struck us as resembling an African Bushman. Anthropologists consulted by the Peabody agreed. But what would a Bushman have been doing in Philadelphia in the 1840's?

Contributing unwittingly to the march of science—or pseudo science—seems to be the answer. In February, 1848, Dr. Samuel Morton, Agassiz' collaborator, exhibited before the Academy of Natural Sciences in Philadelphia a live, eighteen-year-old "Bushman . . . boy," brought to the city "under the kind and paternal auspices of Capt. Chase, United States Consul at the Cape of Good Hope."

In his address, Morton described the boy's curious complexion (the color of a "dried leaf"), his small nose ("so flat as to scarcely be seen in profile"), and his extraordinary tufted hair ("each hair [having] the appearance of an ordinary steel watch spring").

Since Morton and Agassiz often exchanged their latest findings, it seems safe to assume that the boy shown here, thousands of miles from his homeland, was Dr. Morton's celebrated exhibit.

Philadelphia visitor, 1848

Right: Nauvoo, Illinois, in 1846

MORMON MEMORANDA

Since the publication of Rodman Paul's "The Mormons" in our June, 1977, issue, we have learned of a couple of interesting sidelights. The first concerns Nauvoo, the Illinois town from which the beleaguered Mormons fled for the safety of the West in 1844. In April of this year, one Walter Pearce was successful in his second attempt to become Nauvoo's mayor. He was, it is reported, glad that religion was not an issue in the campaign. The point was well taken; Mayor Pearce is a Mormon.

Secondly, it will be remembered that in a sidebar to Professor Paul's article, we discussed the vast genealogical vault that the Church of Jesus Christ of Latter-day Saints (the Mormons) maintains in the Wasatch Mountains of Utah—the largest such facility in the world. Church officials recently dug into those records and came up with a genealogy for President Jimmy Carter, tracking his family down for twelve generations. In accepting the unexpected offering from Church leaders, the President remarked that "We've uncovered some embarrassing ancestors in the not-too-distant past. Some horse thieves, and some people killed on Saturday nights. One of my relatives, unfortunately, was even in the newspaper business."

THE LOVE OF WAMPUM WAS THE ROOT OF ALL EVIL

A little over three hundred years ago, according to an intriguing new theory, the cluster of Dutch settlements that was to become New York City was brought to its financial knees—not by uncontrolled welfare costs, increased labor costs, budgetary bungling, or general mismanagement, but by small beads no more than 9.5 millimeters long and 3.2 millimeters in diameter. Strung together in six-foot lengths (called fathoms), these tiny ornaments, in the view of anthropologist Lynn Ceci of Queens College, New York, were a major cause not only of the Pequot Indian War of the 1630's but also of a great wampum crisis of the 1660's that ended in Dutch New Amsterdam's becoming British New York without a shot being fired.

For the beads were wampum, which is to say, money, and for a time wampum, backed by the "Fur Standard," was the principal medium of exchange in a region that had little other coinage. Most of the beads were made from certain mollusk shells by coastal tribes from Rhode Island to New Jersey and traded to the Dutch of New Amsterdam and the English of New England for cloth and other European goods. The whites then used the wampum to buy furs from the Iroquois and other inland tribes who valued the beads.

In 1637, when the Pequots of Connect-icut had established control over many of the wampum-making tribes, the British, according to Ceci's new interpretation, launched war against the Pequots to seize control of the source of the wealth for themselves. They were successful, and the consequent availability of large amounts of cheap wampum in their own hands gave the New Englanders a great advantage over their Dutch fur-trading rivals. That advantage was strengthened in 1652 when the Massachusetts Bay Colony began minting the pine tree shilling, which quickly replaced wampum as the medium of exchange among the British colonies. These were only too happy, however, to use wampum in trading with the Dutch, and the result was inflation of profound dimensions as the British "dumped" thousands of fathoms of wampum into the Dutch economy. "Dutch farmers, laborers, and soldiers," Ceci notes, "were impoverished as the cost of goods and wages soared in New Amsterdam, the price of bread and shoes, for example, rising as much as 400 percent."

By the 1660's New Amsterdam was staggering, and when the Duke of York decided to seize the territory in 1664, the Dutch were helpless to resist. New Amsterdam thus became New York—the creation of a bunch of beads.

HE IS WHAT HE ATE

Our little feature on diners, "Slice of Pie and a Cup of Coffee—That'll Be Fifteen Cents, Honey," in the April, 1977, issue brought forth a note of commendation from Fred E. Magel of River Forest, Illinois. Mr. Magel knows whereof he speaks, for he tells us that "My father was a restaurant buff and a builder. I served the late Duncan Hines grading key restaurants. Perhaps I've dined in more restaurants than anyone else in history."

That is entirely possible, since Mr. Magel has eaten in more than forty thousand restaurants and is listed as the champion restaurant patron in the *Guinness Book of Records*. "I'm the only one in the book," he tells us, "who breaks his own record *daily*."

Iroquois leaders with Wampum. An enlarged view of a wampum belt is in the foreground.

OF CRUEL AND UNUSUAL DEATH SENTENCES

One hardly expects to find flights of slightly demented rhetoric in the words a judge uses to sentence a convicted felon. However, there are exceptions.

Take, for example, a diatribe said to have been delivered by Judge M. B. Gerry when sentencing Alferd E. Packer to death for having killed and eaten five companions while caught in a Colorado blizzard in 1873. (See "Postscripts" for the April, 1977, issue.) "Stand up, you man-eating son-of-a-bitch, and receive your sentence!" Judge Gerry reportedly began. "There were seven Democrats in Hinsdale County, but you, you voracious, man-eating son-of-a-bitch, you ate five of them. I sentence you to be hanged by the neck until you're dead, dead, dead, as a warning against reducing the Democratic population of the state."

Judge Gerry's outburst was probably apocryphal, but we have found another death sentence from the same era that is equally bizarre but apparently authentic. It was delivered in 1881:

"José Manuel Miguel Xavier Gonzales, in a few short weeks, it will be spring. The snows of winter will flee away, the ice will vanish, and the air will become soft and balmy. In short, José Manuel Miguel Xavier Gonzales, the annual miracle of the years will awaken and come to pass, but you won't be there.

"The rivulet will run its soaring course to the sea, the timid desert flowers will put forth their tender shoots, the glorious valleys of this imperial domain will blossom as the rose. Still, you won't be here to see.

"From every tree top some wild woods songster will carol his mating song, butterflies will sport in the sunshine, the busy bee will hum happy as it pursues its accustomed vocation. The gentle breeze will tease the tassels of the wild grasses, and all nature, José Manuel Miguel Xavier Gonzales, will be glad but you. You won't be here to enjoy it because I command the sheriff or some other officer of this country to lead you out to some remote spot, swing you by the neck from a knotting bough of a sturdy oak, and let you hang until you are dead.

"And then, José Manuel Miguel Xavier Gonzales, I further command that such officer or officers retire quickly from your dangling corpse, that vultures may descend from the heavens upon your filthy body until nothing shall remain but bare, bleached bones of a cold-blooded, copper-colored, blood-thirsty, throat-cutting, chili-eating, sheep-herding, murdering son-of-a-bitch."

We have no information about the frustrated bard of a judge who composed this, or of the unfortunate José Manuel Miguel Xavier Gonzales. We asked the editors of *Antaeus* magazine, in whose Autumn, 1976, issue we found the sentence, but they had no information other than that the case was *United States of America v. Gonzales* (1881), United States District Court, New Mexico Territory Sessions. We couldn't find it, but perhaps some of our readers might know of it.

```
B O L A   W A G O N   W A I N S     B A D
A M O R   A P U R O   E R N I E   C O L O
N A N A   Y E L L O W S T O N E   O N I T
C R E D O S   P O S I T   N E G A U N E E
    R O O T S   S E N O R   R A N G E
T E A S H O P S   D E F O E   R E A V E R
R A N   S P L A T   S T U N G   T R I P E
E R G O   S I G H T   H E A R S   S L E D
S E E M S   T E E H E E   M A T E   L E O
  D R A W L S   B E E P S   N E C H E S
    H I E R   A G L E T   D A L E
  S H A S T A   G R E C O   C L A M P S
A P O   S U I T   E R O I C A   T A L A R
C A R P   P L A T A   S C A N S   N A N O
R I S E S   S M I T H   S L Y A S   I T A
E N E R O S   P E D A L   M O N T A N A N
  O F O U R   D I V E S   N I L E S
D E P U T I E S   V E G A S   C O N F E R
E L E M   S I T T I N G B U L L   E O L A
E I R E   S N E R D   E L S I E   A L L I
R E A   E S T E E   D E A L S   S K E D
```

Solution to the August
Crossword Puzzle